TO THE MEMORY OF THE FALLEN.

WE KNOW IT WASN'T YOUR FAULT.

WE REMEMBER YOU WITH LOVE.

CONTENTS

‘OUR FIRST JOB
IS SURVIVAL.
IF WE SURVIVE,
WE LEARN.

WHEN WE LEARN,
WE MAKE TOMORROW
BETTER THAN TODAY.

THAT’S WHAT IT MEANS
TO BE HUMAN.

WE JUST HAVE TO
KEEP ON GOING.’

**GRAFFITI FOUND IN THE
WRECKAGE OF DOWNPATRICK**

INTRODUCTION

WHAT IS THIS BOOK FOR?

THESE DAYS ARE THE WORST ANY OF US HAVE EVER SEEN.

Our best estimate is that over 90 per cent of the population of the United Kingdom is dead or, worse, has joined the ranks of the living dead. None of us needs to be reminded of the horrors we have seen. All of us have at times thought that we were witnessing, as H. G. Wells put it, 'the rout of civilization . . . the massacre of mankind'. And yet, here we stand. If you are reading this book, you are one of the survivors. Humanity has not yet passed from the earth.

Why, in these terrible days, have we produced a guide to health, fitness and wellbeing? It is because we believe fundamentally that this is not the end. Whatever your situation today, however bad things are, we believe that measured, repeated and committed effort can improve things. You can work to make your life better.

And you are not alone. We have produced this guide, and we have delivered it by hand and via airdrop to every area of the country we can reach, because we want you to know that we are with you. This is a basic truth in the post-zombie world: whatever you do to improve your own health and wellbeing improves the lot of everyone. Whatever you do to help yourself, you help all of us.

We, the community of living humans who remain, cannot do without you. We want you to succeed in your endeavours, whether you are growing your own crops, improving your walking speed or constructing a zombie-proof chicken coop. Each of us is striving every day to build a new world from the ashes of the old.

WE WANT YOU WITH US.

INTRODUCTION

WHAT IS THE MINISTRY OF RECOVERY?

Although the Ministry is operating as the only quasi-governmental force in the United Kingdom, it is important to make our position clear.

We are not the elected government of this country. Until there are elections, there is no democratically elected government of the United Kingdom. The throne of the United Kingdom is also currently empty, following the tragic events at Balmoral, although we are working to trace any distant relatives of the Royal Family who may remain alive. The Minister for Recovery, Sigrid Hakkinen, is the most senior civil servant who is known to have survived; we would be grateful to have knowledge of any other senior members of government who survived the massacre in the Downing Street bunker.

The Ministry of Recovery is mostly composed of people who worked in government and in government-funded organizations before the apocalypse. Some of us were civil servants; a number of us worked for the Ministry of Defence, which was able to save many of its people; some of us worked for the National Health Service, in local government or for the BBC. Some of us were in position throughout the first weeks of the apocalypse, securing some vital services such as water and communications, or ensuring the orderly shutdown of nuclear power stations and weapons.

Collectively, we had access to a great deal of knowledge about how the United Kingdom runs, we knew where various resources were held, and had, in some cases, access to classified information. We are doing our best to use our knowledge and skills for the good of the country in these unprecedented times. For most of us, no training or emergency procedure instructions that we have ever been given covers anything like this.

We know that what we're doing is not enough. Nothing could ever be enough. But we're trying to use what we have to help. This guide is for the living people who remain, and consists of the best knowledge and advice we have to give. Whatever resources you have available, there will be a way to use them to make your life a little better. That is our hope for you.

SECTION 01

THE HOME FRONT

THE HOME FRONT

INTRODUCTORY REMARKS

Each of us has escaped from the zombies, not once but many times. If you are reading this book, you have probably seen someone you love turn grey. You have run from the shambling dead. If you are reading this book, you have witnessed the bite that festers, you have heard the cough that turns into a long moan, you have seen with your own eyes how they chase after us unceasingly, even when their limbs are ragged, their joints are ripped open, their feet are gone.

But you survived, as we all did. In all probability, you found somewhere to take shelter until the zombie horde lost interest in you and moved on.

This book is intended to help you from that moment on. This section, in particular, is aimed at you if you are currently experiencing a siege, or to help you learn what to do if you come under siege in future. As we all know too well now, even the safest of dwelling places can fall prey to attack by a horde. Perhaps you find yourself sheltering on the top floor of an abandoned hotel, the stairs chopped away with an axe, while the mouldering corpses of former guests mill about in the hospitality suite below you. Perhaps you are in your own home and have retrieved an air-dropped copy of this book from the roof of your garage while the moaning dead tried to pull you down to become one of them. Perhaps you thought you were safe trekking into the mountains to herd wild sheep, but have become trapped in an isolated cabin with little hope of seeing a living human face again.

Our research has shown that most zombie sieges last for three days or fewer, and that most survivors will experience an average of four siege situations during a single year in a zombie-infested country. Take heart: if your shelter has survived the first 24 hours of zombie assault, you will probably make it out alive. But even a short siege can be exhausting, and of course we all fear the siege that goes on for months.

Whatever your circumstances, this first section will help you to make the best of the situation. If you are safe now, there is every possibility you will survive. You have already shown your resourcefulness and tenacity. Hordes do move on, or rot into immobility. When the horde that has you pinned down now is gone, you will be grateful that you spent these days, weeks or months improving your physical fitness and keeping to a regular schedule to preserve your mental health.

The human race needs you to survive. Begin today, do as much as you can, and be inspired by your progress day by day and week by week. The zombie apocalypse need not spell the end for all of us. And you are not alone. In the form of this book, we are with you. YOU WILL SURVIVE.

FITNESS BY SETTING UP DEFENCES

We hope that you have already ensured that your dwelling place is as secure as it can be. You are best placed to assess the risks to your life and to decide how to combat them, but Ministry Briefing no. 23: Siege: How to Survive the First 24 Hours will give you useful strategies.

In this guide, our focus is mainly on improving your health and wellbeing. But there are many tasks which perform several functions at once. Traditionally, fitness goals have been split up into three pillars: cardiovascular fitness, strength training and flexibility. Some of the exercises we suggest in this section will have only one of these three aims, but many exercises and zombie-proofing chores will do all three, as well as keeping you safer from zombie attack. Your first job should be to run through this checklist of tasks which will make you safer and also help you on your journey to fitness.

If you are in imminent danger of zombie attack, adrenaline will be racing around your body, giving you more strength, speed and agility than normal. These tasks should all be achievable:

- Leave no ground-floor window uncovered. Nail boards across windows and doors. Zombies tend to press heavily on the exterior of buildings and hinges can often be vulnerable. They will redouble their attacks if they see a living human within. If you have no boards, pile up furniture in front of windows and doors. Be sure to bend your knees and lift with your legs, keeping your back straight.

- Reinforce interior doors with any materials you have available. This may buy you valuable minutes in the event of a home incursion.

- If you are in a position to do so, erect a fence – even a lowish chain-link fence will hold back a horde for hours or days.

- Gather your supplies in the upstairs area, if you have one, or wherever you have identified as the safest hiding place in your dwelling. Keeping your supplies in one place will help you to keep track of them, and you will have no fear that if you need to retreat you will end up leaving vital supplies behind.

(Continued overleaf)

(Continued from previous page)

- If there is a danger of zombies getting in, and if there is an upper floor to retreat to, destroy the staircase with axes. Work from the bottom, going up, and be sure to leave yourself a safe way of reaching the ground floor when the horde has passed on, even if it's only a knotted rope of sheets.

- If you are intending to shelter in an upstairs area or on the roof of a property as a last resort, begin to construct an escape route, perhaps to a neighbouring roof, and practise using it. Many people have escaped from dangerous situations using equipment as simple as a knotted-sheet rope and a grappling hook fashioned from metal bed struts. Time spent learning to throw and aim well is never wasted.

WHY TRY TO KEEP FIT DURING A LONG SIEGE?

It can be tempting to give in to despair. We have all done so at times. The days are endless and the nights are devastating. The losses are unbearable. The pain is measureless. What reason could there possibly be to perform step-ups on a bottom stair or lift a filled kettle to build upper-body strength?

But consider this:

- **Despair is often a function of inactivity.** When you sit immobile in your dwelling place all day, watching the rotting faces of the dead through your window, you will become depressed. Moving around more will almost certainly give you more energy. It is worth a go, is it not, before you give up all hope in a bright future for humanity?

- **You will see an improvement in a fairly short space of time.** This will also help you to feel that hope remains. When you notice that you can lift a heavier backpack full of books, or that you can fend off attack from a well-rotted zombie without becoming winded, you will remember that things can get better, even now.

- **You won't be besieged forever.** When you escape, you'll be glad of your ability to sprint away from zombies, to throw heavy things at them, to carry a full backpack of supplies to your next home, to climb a tree or a fence, to wield a weapon successfully. And exercising with this in mind will help you to believe that escape is possible.

- **We need you.** Other humans need you. You are not alone; we will help you however we can. But you have responsibilities too. Your responsibility to all the other human beings who have worked and struggled to survive until today is to stay alive too. Do whatever you can do.

- **Whatever you do has value.** There are communities out there waiting for you to join them after you make your escape. They will be grateful if you can carry water or fight or rock an infant. Whatever you do to improve your own fitness, you do for all of us.

And we thank you.

MY REASONS TO SURVIVE THIS APOCALYPSE:

1) ....

....

....

2) ....

....

....

3) ....

....

....

4) ....

....

....

5) ....

....

....

INDOOR CARDIOVASCULAR ROUTINE FOR BEGINNERS

As we all know, it is essential to keep quiet inside your home or hiding place during a siege. Persistent loud noises suggesting living humans are inside the home will encourage the zombies outside to pay attention. They may then start up a long 'hunting' or 'hunger' moan, which will draw further undead to their forces, and they may be encouraged to renew their attacks on your home, putting pressure on windows or doors. We have therefore suggested activities to raise your heart rate which can be accomplished quietly, without jumping or stepping heavily.

When starting an indoor cardiovascular programme, begin slowly. You probably do not have access to a doctor to treat you if you make yourself unwell. Listen to your body. Stretch your muscles before and after your workout (see page 35) to prevent injury and soreness. If you have not exercised recently, begin with five minutes of movement that makes you slightly warm and breathe more quickly (make sure you have enough breath left to shout for help if necessary!). Add one minute every few days to this routine until you are able to perform gentle exercise for half an hour.

- Try stepping on and off the bottom stair in your property, if you have stairs. This is particularly recommended if your stairs are carpeted and you are unlikely to make too much noise as you do this.

- Gently walk or dance on the spot – be aware of noise, but if you have a well-carpeted room or one without windows, you can perform low-impact dance moves such as the grapevine step, high-knee walking and leg-kicks. Punching the air while exercising will increase your heart rate and help to improve cardiovascular fitness.

- Squats are a powerful exercise which increase muscle strength in your legs and bottom as well as raising your heart rate. Be careful not to squat down too far, and keep the knees in line with the ankles. The movement you're aiming for is as if you were about to sit down in a chair: those new to exercise may like to begin simply by sitting in a chair and standing up ten times without holding on to the chair's arms or anything else. Build up in sets of ten as you feel able. You could also modify this exercise by performing it against a wall, sliding up and down, using the wall to support some of your weight.

Mr G-V of Tottenham tells us:

'Before the apocalypse, I hadn't paid much attention to exercise, to be honest. Just commuting into Central London every day was exhausting enough and I used to collapse on the sofa every evening. But after the fall of London, I was stuck in my third-floor maisonette for eight weeks – I thought I might be there forever! The only thing that kept me sane was my workout routine.

'I started by just trying out some push-ups and walking on the spot. It was a real buzz to notice my muscles getting stronger, and it took my mind off the undead bodies of my decomposing neighbours growling outside.

'By week seven I found I was strong enough – and light enough! – to pull myself up on to the roof of the building. From there, I could signal for help and was rescued by the military police.'

INDOOR CARDIOVASCULAR ROUTINE FOR IMPROVERS

Try out both of these exercises and see if you can do ten repetitions without stopping. Also ensure that you enjoy the exercises and do not do anything that you think is beyond your current strength and ability – you must keep enough reserves of energy that you are able to flee for your life if need be! And of course make sure that the exercises do not make too much noise, attracting zombie attention!

Then, three to five times a week, pick five of the exercises and perform several rounds of either ten repetitions or one minute of each exercise, with a short rest between each set. You should aim to build up to 30 minutes of exercise per session. Although we have designated these exercises as 'cardiovascular' training, many of them will also enhance your strength. For example, any exercise that involves straightening your legs or hips against resistance (including bodyweight) will strengthen the muscles in your legs.

We have provided a chart on pages 24 and 25 for you to fill in which exercises you do on which days, with notes on your performance, progress, and how each exercise felt.

LIST OF TASKS TO REINFORCE MY HOME:

1) ....

....

2) ....

....

3) ....

....

4) ....

....

5) ....

....

6) ....

....

7) ....

....

8) ....

....

MAKE SURE THAT THE EXERCISES DO NOT MAKE TOO MUCH NOISE, ATTRACTING ZOMBIE ATTENTION!

LESS CHALLENGING EXERCISES

- **One minute bodyweight squats**
  Stand upright with your arms by your sides and your legs hip-distance apart. Squat down as if you were about to sit in a chair – take care that your knees don't come out further than your feet as you squat; your bottom should be sticking out! Stand up again. Repeat. Use a wall to slide down if you need this support.

- **One minute dead-bug walking**
  Lie on your back with your arms and legs in the air – like a dying bug! 'Walk' your arms and legs in the air for one minute as rapidly as you can without becoming out of breath.

- **One minute high-knee walking, with arms up**
  March on the spot for one minute, pumping your arms vigorously and aiming to bring your knees to waist height with each step.

- **One minute punching the air**
  Hold your arms in front of you in the 'fighting stance' – one fist protecting your face while the other is more extended for an attack. Then punch the air for one minute, being careful not to fully extend or lock your elbows. You may like to vary this exercise by punching a pillow for one minute. Never attempt to punch a zombie without protection for your fists – a direct face-punch with bare fists is very likely to end in infection.

- **One minute stepping on and off the bottom stair**
  Step on and off the bottom stair in your home for one minute. You may be surprised how challenging this can be – you can increase the pace as you become fitter. Stairs will always be a good fitness resource, as long as you do not have to destroy them to stop an encroaching zombie horde from reaching you on a high floor of your dwelling.

REMEMBER THAT WHATEVER YOU'RE DOING WILL INCREASE YOUR FITNESS, AND THAT THERE IS NO PARTICULAR STANDARD YOU SHOULD MEET!

BODYWEIGHT
SQUATS

BODYWEIGHT
SQUATS (BEGINNER)

FORTIFYING
A DOOR

HIGH-KNEE WALKING

STAIRS

MORE CHALLENGING EXERCISES

Proceed with caution with these exercises; if you have painful hips or knees, or problems with your shoulders, you would be well advised to stick to the less-challenging exercises. The zombie apocalypse is an inopportune time to aggravate any existing injury or joint problem!

- **Ten jumping jacks**
  Stand upright with your arms by your sides and your legs together. Jump into a 'star' shape – with your arms outstretched and your legs apart. Then jump back to your starting position. This is one jumping jack.

- **Five mountain climbers**
  Get down on to the floor, and support your weight on your arms (as in a push-up or plank position) and the toes of one outstretched leg and one bent leg. In one movement, switch legs, so that the outstretched leg is bent and the bent leg is stretched out. Jump back to your starting position. This is one mountain climber.

- **Five burpees**
  Stand upright with your hands by your sides. Then crouch down, lean forward, support your weight on your arms, and jump your legs back together so that you are in a full 'push-up' position. Then jump your legs forward, so that you are crouching again. Then stand up. This is one burpee.

- **Ten tuck jumps**
  Stand upright with your arms by your sides and your legs hip-distance apart, with knees slightly bent. Jump up, bringing both knees as high as you can in front of you while still being able to comfortably return to a standing position. This is one tuck jump.

- **One minute running with cans**
  Hold a food can in each hand – make sure that you can grip them without dropping them on your toes! Run on the spot for one minute, swinging your arms to increase your cardio challenge.

As you become even fitter, you should start to decrease the rest period between each exercise, aiming eventually for the rest period to be a maximum of ten seconds. Once the exercises start to feel easy to you, increase the number of repetitions by one repetition per week, or the amount of time by ten seconds per week.

Once you are able to complete 20 repetitions or three minutes of continuous exercise for each activity, you can begin to increase the number of rounds of exercises you perform. Do not be concerned if you never reach this level; three minutes of burpees, for example, is a challenge for all but the very fittest.

LESS CHALLENGING EXERCISES						
DATE	Bodyweight squats	Dead-bug walking	High-knee walking	Punching the air	Stepping on stairs	Notes and modifications

MORE CHALLENGING EXERCISES						
DATE	Jumping jacks	Mountain climbers	Burpees	Tuck jumps	Running with cans	Notes and modifications

MY EXERCISE ROUTINES

MY EXERCISE ROUTINES

INDOOR STRENGTH ROUTINE FOR BEGINNERS

The most useful strength routine is one which will enable you to flee more effectively and to fight for your life with a greater degree of success.

A simple strength routine you can do at home is outlined below. Perform it two or three days a week, with a rest day in between each training session to allow your muscles time to recover. Remember to begin slowly and not to strain your muscles too much. We have provided a chart overleaf for you to record your exercise sessions and chart your progress.

Work up to being able to perform three rounds of:

- **Ten chair dips**
  Sit on a sturdy, armless chair with your feet flat on the ground and your hands placed palm down on the seat either side of you. Now slide your bottom off the chair and raise yourself up and down using your arms. Those with shoulder problems should start with press-ups against a wall.
  Next step as you start to improve and the exercise begins to feel easier: move your feet further away.

- **Ten table-top pull-ups**
  Lie face-up underneath a sturdy table, on your back with your knees bent. Make sure there is no chance you could pull the table over – it must be very stable and well grounded. Grab on to the edge of the table with both hands, with your fingers on top of the table and your palms underneath. Keeping your knees bent, use your arms to raise and lower yourself.
  Next step as you start to improve and the exercise begins to feel easier: move your feet further away.

- **Ten 'seated' knee raises**
  In the corner of a kitchen countertop, or between two sturdy tables, place your palms flat on a stable surface and raise your feet off the floor, supporting yourself with your hands. Now bend your knees and hips so that you are in a 'seated' position, before returning your feet to the floor.
  Next step as you start to improve and the exercise begins to feel easier: extend your legs out and tap the ground with your heels.

- **Ten modified push-ups (on knees, on a chair, or against a wall)**
  A standard push-up is performed by supporting your weight on your hands and tiptoes and raising and lowering yourself using your arms.

  Push-ups can be modified for different abilities and strength levels by:

  - bending your legs and supporting your weight on your knees and lower legs as well as your arms;
  - performing the push-up against a wall; or supporting your upper body on a sturdy chair, rather than on the floor.

  Experiment with these modifications until you find one that is both comfortable and challenging for your body.

- **Thirty-second plank**
  Support yourself in 'push-up' position, resting your weight on your upper arms from elbow to hands, rather than just on your hands. Maintain muscle control in your abdomen so that you do not strain your lower back, and keep your back straight.
  Next step as you start to improve and the exercise begins to feel easier: increase your holding time by 10 seconds a week.

INDOOR STRENGTH ROUTINE FOR BEGINNERS						
DATE	Chair dips	Table-top pull-ups	'Seated' knee raises	Modified push-ups	Plank	Notes and modifications

INDOOR STRENGTH ROUTINE FOR BEGINNERS

DATE	Chair dips	Table-top pull-ups	'Seated' knee raises	Modified push-ups	Plank	Notes and modifications

STRETCHING: WHY IS IT IMPORTANT IN THE ZOMBIE APOCALYPSE?

This is one part of your fitness routine you may be tempted to skip! It's obvious that being able to run, fight and carry supplies is very useful in our fight for survival, but stretching and flexibility? Surely these aren't really necessary?

Consider, though, the words of JT of Peebles, Scotland.

'I'd never been what you'd call fit,' says JT, 'but I always liked my yoga – we did classes down the community centre every Tuesday morning. I just thought it was relaxing. When the zombies came, I thought I was dead for sure. I live in a ground-floor flat, you see, on a council estate, and I had nowhere safe to hide. The gas man turned zombie as he was reading my meter! I ran and hid in the bedroom – he was bashing on the door and I knew he'd get in any minute. I looked around . . . and I thought I'd try hiding in the top of my wardrobe. It was only a wee space, but I squeezed into it, my knees right up against my chest. I waited till he broke through, and then from my safe hiding place I hit him on the head with the curtain pole until his brain smashed all over him!'

You can never be too physically fit for the zombie apocalypse, whether it be in strength, stamina, energy or flexibility. And many of us find joy in doing the very human movements of stretching and flexing – zombie joints begin to stiffen almost immediately post-mortem, giving them their distinctive locked-knee shuffle. So every stretch and bend we do reasserts our own humanity.

If you have not previously been active, we suggest that you not worry overmuch about honing a specific cardiovascular and strength routine. It is likely that strength exercises will make you breathe more heavily and so improve your heart and lung function. And it's also likely that many of the cardiovascular exercises we've suggested will begin to build more muscle on your arms and legs and in your core. Any of the exercises in this book, done on a regular basis, will make you feel fitter, healthier and more able to survive the long, slow death of civilization. Create a routine that is sustainable for you, and keep at it.

FLEXIBILITY ROUTINE FOR BEGINNERS: MORNING MOBILITY

When you wake up in the morning, your muscles and joints haven't moved a great deal for several hours. In the best of circumstances, you may find that you're stiff, sore and in need of a good stretch. And most of us haven't been sleeping in the best circumstances. You may be sleeping on the floor, or in cramped quarters. So start your day off right: with gentle stretching that will increase your mobility and ease stiffness. Remember never to force a movement or perform it if it's painful; always stretch gently and listen to your body's signals about its natural range of movement.

Perform each of these loosening-up exercises and stretches for 30 seconds:

Neck movements: gently roll your head in half-circles clockwise and anti-clockwise. Slowly tip your head forward and back, then side to side, returning to the central position in between.

Wrist movements: keep your elbows still and tucked in by your sides. Circle your wrists clockwise and anti-clockwise. Bend your wrists, pulling your fingers gently towards your inner wrist and then towards the back of your wrists.

Arm circles: hold your arms out at 90 degrees from your body and gently circle clockwise and anti-clockwise.

Cat/cow stretches: kneel on all fours. Push up from your midriff and let your head naturally drop down so you're looking at your knees for the 'cat' stretch. Then bring your head up and arch your back for the 'cow' stretch. Do not move too quickly or with a jerking motion.

Ski jumpers: stand with your arms above your head. Bend your knees and bring your arms down quickly, as if you were pushing off with skis. Return to the starting position. As well as increasing mobility, this exercise should get your blood pumping!

Leg swings: stand with your arms by your side and knees gently bent. Stand on one leg and lift your other leg forwards, then backwards, then out to the side. These should be gentle movements, without ballistic force.

Front stretch: sit on the floor with your legs out in front of you. Touch your toes – or get as near as you can while keeping your spine straight rather than curved – then gently return to the upright position.

Side stretch: sit on the floor with your legs splayed open in a V shape. Touch the toes of your right foot with your left hand – or as near as you can get! – and then the toes of your left foot with your right hand.

IF YOU CAN DO NOTHING ELSE IN THIS BOOK, JUST PERFORMING THESE STRETCHES EVERY MORNING WILL HELP YOUR BODY TO BE AT ITS BEST FOR SURVIVAL.

BALANCE EXERCISES

THE LAST THING YOU WANT WHEN FLEEING FROM ZOMBIE ATTACK IS TO BE IN DANGER OF LOSING YOUR BALANCE OR FALLING OVER!

We recommend improving your balance – particularly if you know it to be weak – by the use of the following exercises.

1. Stand on one leg. If this is hard for you at first, you can touch the wall with your fingertips, but then try to progress to just using one finger and then to not touching the wall at all.

2. Lift your leg to the side, to the front and backwards, without holding on.

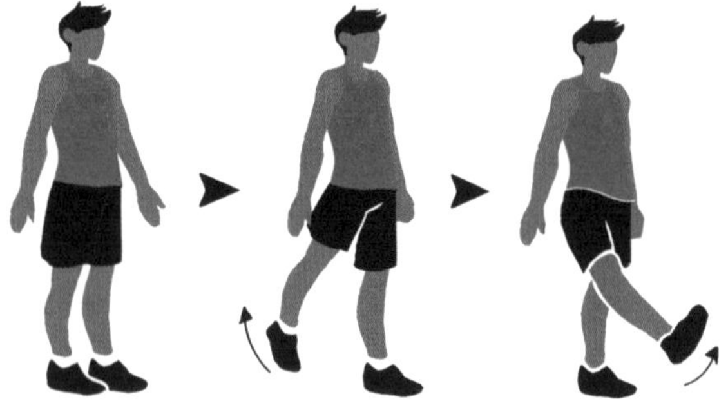

3. Stand on tiptoes while you do routine tasks, such as discussing crop rotations or listening to a Ministry zombie-movement forecast. Standing on a pillow or closing your eyes will make standing on tiptoes much more difficult.

To improve your balance further once these exercises have become easy for you, scavenge a 'wobble board' from a fitness shop.

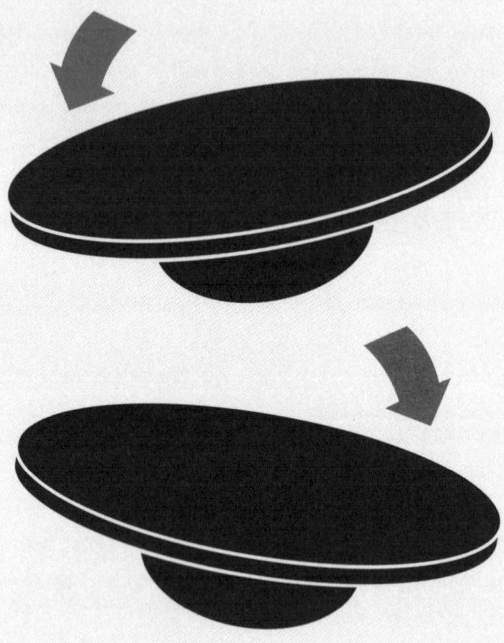

Practise standing on the board until you feel comfortable doing so. Then, for an extra challenge, stand on tiptoes on the board. You may eventually be able to work up to standing on the wobble board on one leg! As ever, please take care with this exercise; if you fall and injure yourself, you will be easy prey for the living dead.

SIMPLE STRETCH ROUTINE FOR AFTER A WORKOUT

After you've performed cardiovascular or strength training, you should take a few moments to stretch out your muscles. This will prevent muscle soreness and mean that you'll be fit to run or fight if necessary even the day after a hard workout. Hold each stretch for a count of 20 to 30. Do not bounce.

- Stretch out each wrist by gently pulling your fingers and hand back towards the back of your wrist, and then forward, towards your inner wrists.
- Stretch your shoulders and upper arms by putting your palm on your back at the base of your neck and then gently pulling on your elbow with the other hand to increase the stretch.
- Stretch your shoulder joints by reaching laterally across your chest with one arm and using the other hand to push the arm closer to your chest.
- Stretch your chest muscles by placing your right arm – bent at a 90-degree angle at the elbow – against a wall, and then rotating your body anti-clockwise until you feel a stretch across your chest. Repeat on the other side.
- Stretch your sides by standing up with your legs hip-distance apart, reaching one arm above your head, and then leaning over to the other side, slowly and under control. Repeat on the opposite side.
- Stretch your stomach muscles by lying flat on your stomach and then using your arms to push your torso up into a 'cobra' position.
- Stretch your hamstrings by standing up, bending one knee and extending the other leg straight out in front of you, with the heel on the ground. Lean forward into the stretch. Repeat with the other leg.
- Stretch out your calf by standing up, bending one leg at the knee and extending the other leg back behind you. Press the heel of the extended leg towards the floor to deepen the stretch. Repeat with the other leg.
- Stretch your thigh muscles by standing up and holding the heel of your right foot behind you in your right hand. Pull gently to stretch out the muscles of the right thigh, pushing your pelvis forward, then repeat on the other side.

WEEKLY PLAN OF ACTIVITIES

We would encourage you to plan out the tasks you would like to accomplish every week. Be realistic. The zombie apocalypse is exceedingly draining, both mentally and physically, and there is little use in setting up a very ambitious training plan only to complete it once and never again. We suggest that you begin with a modest goal of adding three 10–20-minute sessions of gentle exercise into your week. You can increase the number and duration of these sessions once you have become accustomed to fitting them around your survival activities. Use this chart to note the various survival tasks you want to accomplish in a week, and add in your planned exercise sessions.

SATURDAY

SUNDAY

MONDAY
TUESDAY
WEDNESDAY
THURSDAY
FRIDAY

CHORES THAT WILL KEEP YOU FIT

There are a lot of chores to get done in this changed world! While it may be tempting to take as long as possible over your housework to while away the long dark days, it will be better for both your physical and mental health to undertake them briskly. Remember, this conflict will eventually end, and you will feel glad that you made time for reading and self-improvement as well as ensuring that your daily activities kept your heart and muscles strong and healthy.

CLEANING

More important now than ever. A dirty house is a house that may harbour spores of zombie infection. Animals cannot be infected with the virus but rodents and household pets could easily drag infected chunks of flesh into your home. Keep floors and surfaces clean. Tidy up; for an orderly house will help you to feel that the entire world has not plunged into unbearable chaos forever. Sing while you work, or challenge yourself to clean quickly, so that you become slightly breathless.

BURYING YOUR DEAD

If you have any. This is an arduous but necessary task that most of us have had to face at some point. Do not attempt to do this task as quickly as possible – it is easy to pull a muscle and incapacitate yourself for fight or flight – but several hours of digging will improve your cardiovascular fitness. As digging can strain the back, do intersperse your gravedigging with activities that make you stretch, such as cleaning windows of zombie fluids or reinforcing anti-zombie spikes on high walls.

WASHING

Without electricity most of us are washing clothing and bedding by hand. Washing is essential for good hygiene and to prevent the spread of disease. With stocks of antibiotics dwindling, even a previously minor skin infection could prove fatal. Find a clean water supply and wash your clothes and bedding vigorously – this will provide a good workout, thus keeping you healthy in two different ways!

DISPOSING OF WASTE

For most of us, the days of 'taking out the rubbish' are long gone. All tins, paper, glass and plastics can and must be reused. And organic waste should be eaten if edible and composted if not. The Ministry is already sending some exploratory teams to look into mining landfill sites from the time before. However, if you are in possession of hazardous materials or infectious waste, you are requested to quadruple-wrap them in thick plastic and deposit them in Ministry-approved dump sites. If you are not within easy reach of a Ministry-approved dump, do not place these materials in a public waste bin or skip. It is too easy for an animal, zombie or scavenging human to retrieve them. Label them with the hazardous-waste symbol and place them in a locked, cool, dry cupboard in an abandoned house, preferably in an area which is no longer inhabited, and draw the hazardous-waste symbol on the door.

HOW TO KEEP YOUR SPIRITS UP DURING A LONG SIEGE IF ALONE

Solitary isolation has a deleterious effect on the human mind. This is well documented and will affect you too. Do not expect to be immune. Do not consider it weakness of mind or of will if you become depressed, hyper-anxious, experience insomnia or begin to doubt reality. It is not your fault. The siege will end and you will find help. Until then, some recommendations:

If there are stray domesticated animals around which seem friendly and you are able to keep them alive without harming your own chances of survival, their companionship will be the greatest boon to your solitude. Keep a dog, a cat, a gerbil, a fish or even a house plant alive – depending on your resources – to improve your own mood and hopefulness.

Take on a project, of any sort – preferably several projects, including a health and fitness routine. Examples of other projects might include: keeping a small garden with whatever soil and outdoor space you have available; painting, wood-whittling, knitting or any other manual creative activity; reading, perhaps the great works of literature, many of which can be found on ROFFLENET (see Appendix A); completing a course of study, if you have access to the materials – there are many skills which will be critically needed in the post-apocalypse world and work enough for each of us for a lifetime; studying some aspect of zombie behaviour and writing up your observations. The critical thing is not the nature of the project but that you should feel engaged in it and be able to see utility in your own life.

Keep a journal for each project, noting down every day what you did to move towards your various goals. The Ministry is collecting such journals as part of a project to record life on the Home Front during the current emergency; one day, your journal may be the subject of academic study and help future generations to understand what life was like during this time.

Keep to a regular daily schedule – it will make you feel more human. Do not sleep in through the day; we cannot afford to waste daylight. Rise with the dawn and set yourself regular work to accomplish through the day. Feeling useful and active is as much an essential to good health as proper nutrition and exercise. We have included a sample daily routine on pages 46 and 47.

Use ROFFLENET as a companion and the Ministry's regular radio broadcasts, if you have access to electricity and receiving equipment. Both of these systems, if you are able to access them, will punctuate your day and remind you that you are not one person alone but part of a vast civilian force dedicated to maintaining our way of life.

▲ ROFFLENET SYMBOL

HOW TO KEEP YOUR SPIRITS UP DURING A LONG SIEGE IF IN A GROUP

The mere presence of a group of others – even if they are not like-minded company – will protect against the worst effects of a long siege. Members of a group can take turns manning watch-points, fortifying defences, cooking, gathering water and sleeping. It's very common for members of a group to 'get on each other's nerves' – this is normal and, as with the depression common in isolation, it is not your fault. But try to remember that each of the people in your party have probably suffered terrible, almost unimaginable, loss, horror and privation.

Many of the recommendations for the solitary survivor apply, as well as some recommendations particular to the group situation.

- Set up a regular daily and weekly timetable. Insist that every member of the party washes regularly, if possible, and is given equal rations.

- Work together on a project – perhaps a plan for escape or to improve your rain-catching devices. Each of you should contribute. Every survivor can always offer something. Allow time for personal projects.

- If possible, allot each survivor an area of expertise to read about and study – anything from the basics of plumbing or electricity to Renaissance art will be useful and interesting to other survivors once your siege is over.

- If you are engaged in physical labour together, you might consider choosing the person with the best reading voice to read a novel or other book to the group while you work. This will give you the sense of exploring a story together – like watching TV dramas in the time before – something to talk over in your rest periods, and exchange theories about. Be careful that these discussions do not become too heated!

- If at all possible, give each member of the group some private time alone. You may designate a certain room as the 'alone time' space. We have heard of some long single-room sieges in which the group decided by mutual agreement that a certain curtained-off corner was considered 'soundproof' and that any conversations that took place there would be ignored by the others.

- If you are able, give each member of the party a private journal to write in. The privacy of these journals must be sacrosanct. Every person needs to express their own thoughts somehow, and if you are trapped together in a confined space, this need becomes even more pressing.

- Likewise, if you have access to ROFFLENET, never ever read others' messages or mail or tolerate any member of your party doing so.

IDEAS FOR PERSONAL AND GROUP PROJECTS

1) ....

....

2) ....

....

3) ....

....

4) ....

....

5) ....

....

SUNLIGHT

If you're stuck indoors through a long siege, make sure you regularly expose your skin to sunlight, so that your body can manufacture Vitamin D. If you're in a normal home, you can simply stand by a window with the sun falling on your arms and face for at least 15 minutes a day. If you are trapped in an office building, be aware that many office windows are made with polarized glass, which doesn't allow the sun's rays to penetrate in a way that your body can use. If you are able to access the roof, you should use this as a sun-exposure area. Otherwise, if you are trapped by zombies in the middle floors of an abandoned office building, you will have to smash a window – if necessary, board it up after everyone in your party has spent a few minutes in the sun. If you are in a large office building that is well sealed against zombies, you might like to turn one room – or even a whole floor! – into a solarium by removing all the windows. Isolating this area will make it easier to abandon if the zombies get in.

BOOKS

You may have the opportunity to visit a library or bookshop at some point in your zombie survival journey. If you spot any of these books, be sure to loot them. Some of them will provide useful exercise suggestions, while others will remind you that we are not the first to survive terrifying ordeals or isolation.

ALONE
ADMIRAL BYRD

DEEP SURVIVAL: WHO LIVES, WHO DIES, AND WHY
LAURENCE GONZALES

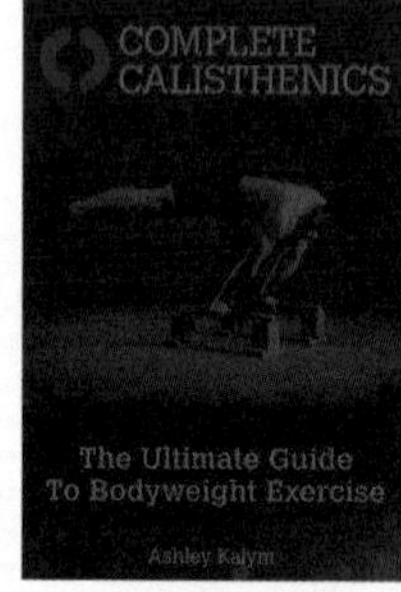

COMPLETE CALISTHENICS: THE ULTIMATE GUIDE TO BODYWEIGHT EXERCISE
ASHLEY KALYM

THE OFFICIAL BRITISH ARMY FITNESS GUIDE
SAM MURPHY

TOUCHING THE VOID
JOE SIMPSON

WILD: FROM LOST TO FOUND ON THE PACIFIC CREST TRAIL
CHERYL STRAYED

EVERY STRETCH AND BEND WE DO ASSERTS OUR HUMANITY

SAMPLE DAILY FITNESS AND WELLNESS ROUTINE

You will know the resources you have available. This timetable is only a sample, and presumes that you have access to a battery-operated radio and some books and other materials. Please do not despair if you don't have access to these things. The most important thing is to create a timetable and stick to it, not the specifics of our suggestions. This timetable is designed to help the solo survivor make it through the difficult weeks of a siege; if you are in a group, you should construct your timetable together, leaving time for communal meals and joint projects.

DAWN	• Wake up. Perform flexibility training and yoga. • Listen to Ministry radio, which provides morning music and entertainment to accompany your exercise routines (see pages 20–35). Eat breakfast. (See the 'Food for Heroes' chapter for advice on food selection, if you have different foods available.) • Examine your perimeter for signs of zombie attack in the night.
MORNING	• Perform any necessary repairs or modifications to zombie defences. • Empty your water-collectors. • Study a book from your collection or read a novel, or work on any other personal project. • Cardiovascular exercise for up to one hour.
MIDDAY	• Eat lunch, if you have any available. • Write in your journal, recording your morning's activities. • If possible, listen to the Ministry's midday radio hour; we are often able to broadcast salvaged BBC programmes from the time before at midday and one hour after dusk.

AFTERNOON	• Perform checks on your security once more, before dusk. • Strength-training exercise, including weapons training and practice if you are in danger of zombie attack. • Take part in some kind of creative project, perhaps decorating objects in your home or drawing in a sketch book. • Reset any perimeter alarms you have set up.
DUSK	• Take a sighting of the zombies at your perimeter, if possible. Note any unusual movements or if the crowd has diminished or increased. Zombies are most active at sunset; if you regularly observe them at this time and make notes, you will notice any changes. • Eat the evening meal while there is still daylight; this is particularly recommended if you are uncertain whether any of your food supplies have spoiled. • Listen to the Ministry broadcast if possible.
NIGHT	• If you have light available, write a journal or read. • We recommend sleeping with earplugs in or headphones over your ears, to combat the sound of the moaning. • If there is no light and you are alone, you might occupy yourself until you sleep by planning a personal project. For example: mentally design your dream zombie-proof house, plan out a novel you would like to write, or decide where in the world you would most like to travel to if it ever becomes possible to leave the country.

YOUR DAILY FITNESS AND WELLNESS ROUTINE

DAWN	
MORNING	
MIDDAY	

AFTERNOON	
DUSK	
NIGHT	

CASE STUDY: Jody Marsh

I used to live on the top floor of one of those green eco-tower-blocks they built on the Thames after the flooding. I loved being up so high, watching the birds flying past the windows, and it was so quiet compared to the city. I even had a little balcony – used to sit out there with my boyfriend in the evenings, watch the sun set over London ... beautiful.

I was really lucky with the apocalypse. I was off sick from work! Five days in bed with flu – actual flu, not grey flu – and I'd ordered in a ton of food and energy drinks from the supermarket. Honestly, I was luckier than most. I saw it on the news first of all, and once I got my binoculars and looked down into the street ... well, after five days there wasn't much doubt it was true.

There were six of us on that top floor of the building – we got together and cleared out the zombies from the other flats on our floor, threw quite a few of them out of the windows! Then we pooled our food, and barricaded ourselves in. We set up little gardens on our balconies and got up on to the roof to do rain collection there.

I must have been there for ... all told about five months, I think. It wasn't easy – after the news went, we felt very isolated – but we didn't get many zombies coming up all those stairs! I grew some pretty good veg out of the seeds I took from my leftovers in the fridge! And we set up one of the other flats on our floor as a gym with weights and that.

We also decided that we'd make a mural together about the people on our floor who'd turned zom or just left and never came back. We turned one massive wall of our corridor into an art piece: we did drawings of them, stuck up things they'd liked. I put my boyfriend's favourite books up there and drew pictures of bands he liked. We all got together to do Mr McKenzie in Flat H, who none of us had known that well. In a funny way, I think it kept us sane, that mural. It felt important, like we were doing something more than just surviving. That we had to keep on going because they deserved a memorial to their lives.

We got rescued in the end – you wouldn't believe me if I told you how! – but I sometimes think about how that mural's probably still up there. Maybe it will be for hundreds of years. And that feels good.

THE HOME FRONT

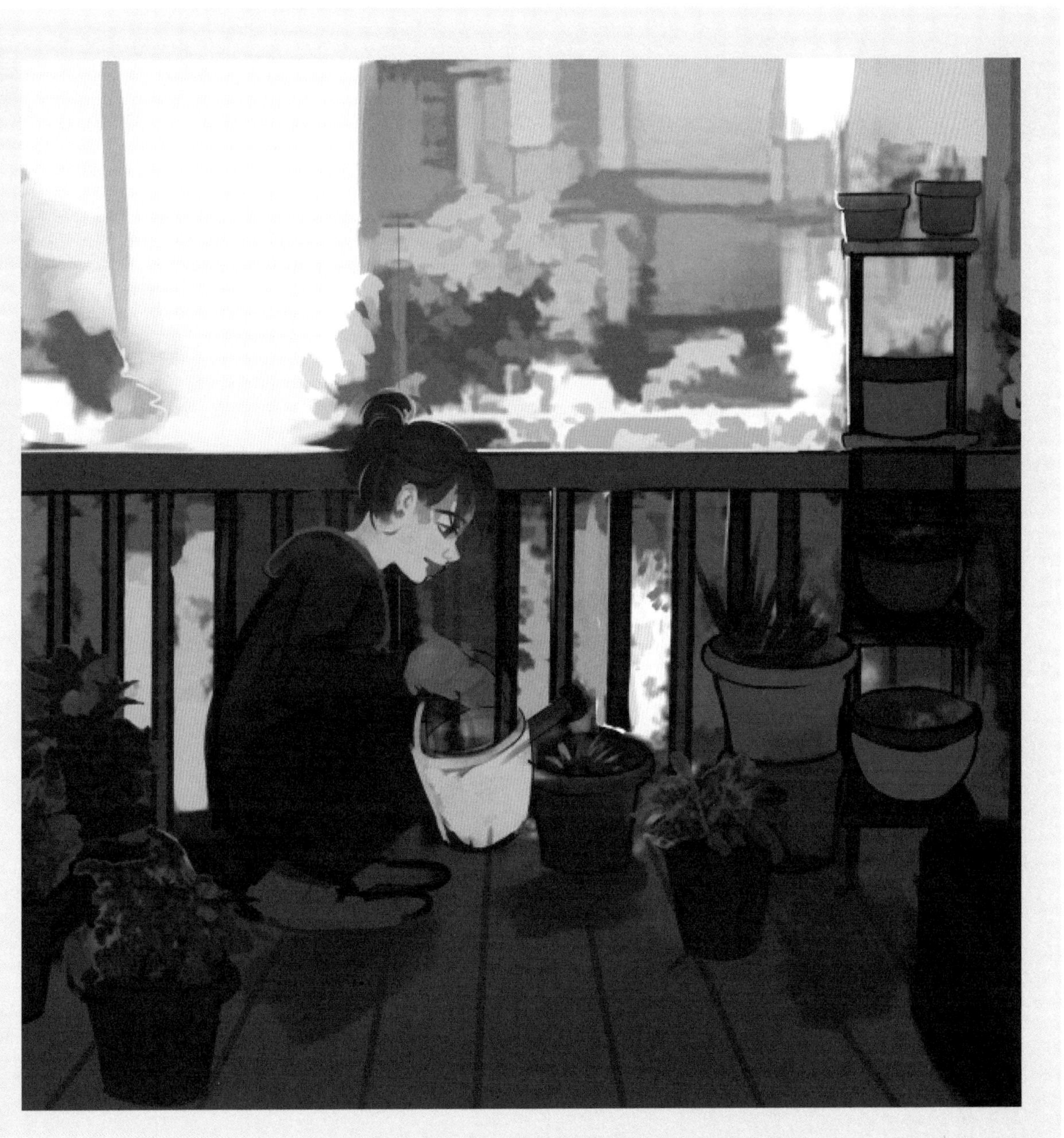

NOTES

VENTURING FORTH

If you have worked through these steps and still feel confident in leaving your home – congratulations! You have successfully survived a siege. Spend the night before you leave planning your route and what you will do the next day. Remember not to leave your home before dawn, and to ensure that you can return well before dusk.

There are exciting possibilities ahead of you and new opportunities, but also new dangers. This section of the book will guide you through the changed landscape of post-zombie Britain and how to stay safe as you navigate this new world.

SCOUTING YOUR LOCAL AREA: WHY AND HOW

For many survivors, life depends on knowing their local area exceedingly well. Most of us will spend several months at least in one place; if we're lucky, we may find a well-defended stronghold where we can expect to live out these emergency years. In either case, the precise disposition of our surroundings means the difference between success and failure in our struggle for life.

CASE STUDY

Consider the case of Mrs S of Merthyr Tydfil, Wales, who, by careful daily examination of her own home and the neighbouring streets, was able to determine that an unusual zombie behaviour – burrowing – was occurring underground. She documented the changes in earthworks, produced detailed sketches and maps. Eventually, she was able to convince her neighbours to band together and dig out the crawler-zombies, who had nearly smashed a hole in the basement of a school housing orphaned children, attracted by the noise of a generator.

Rigorous defences mean constantly paying attention to your environment and being alert to danger. When the dispersal of a zombie horde means that you may leave your home or shelter, you must immediately institute a pattern of regular walks – twice-daily at minimum – through your local neighbourhood to gain a sense of what is 'normal' and what is 'out of place'.

Whether you are in an urban setting or a rural one, the procedure is the same. Called 'quartering', the technique was developed by game-hunters, and can be compared to a person from the time before going up and down the aisles in a supermarket. If you have a map available or can draw one from memory, divide it up into manageable sectors. (If you have no map, your first objective on leaving your place of refuge should be to create one.) Then plot a zigzag path around the area, making sure that you cover every piece of ground, every road, cul-de-sac, every copse of trees, abandoned shopping centre or burned-out petrol garage. Aim to cover every single road or walkable area within one square mile of your shelter every four to five days. In this way, any changes in your neighbourhood will be immediately obvious to you, and you will be able to plan accordingly.

If you have one, a dog will be invaluable in this process and will alert you early to new dangers that you yourself may not be able to detect.

MAP OF MY LOCAL AREA

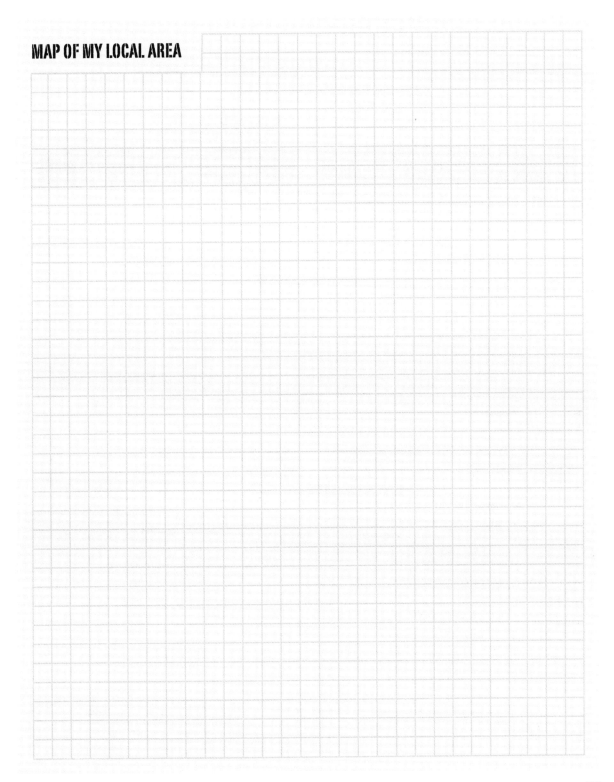

SCOPING THE NEIGHBOURHOOD

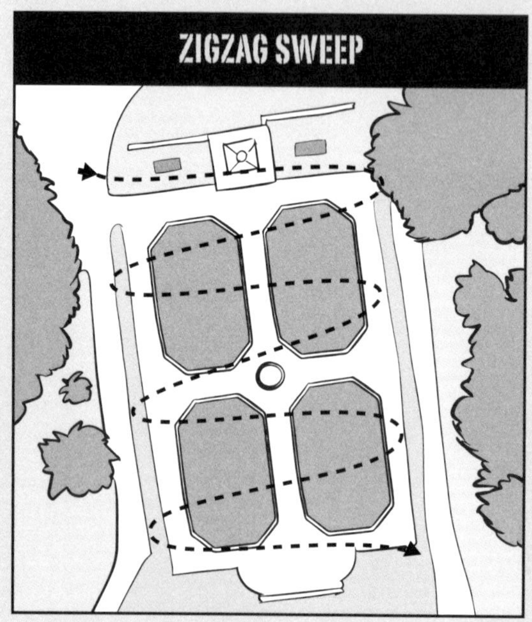

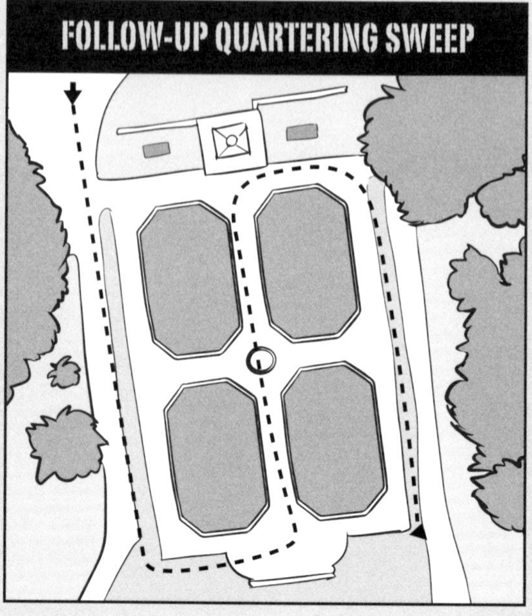

SCOUTING THE LOCAL AREA: WHAT TO LOOK OUT FOR

When you perform your preliminary 'quartering' recce of the area, you should first ensure that you are safe. Are there any zombies? Dangerous animals? Crawlers or zombie body parts that need to be disposed of lest they pose an infection risk?

But once these necessities are taken care of, you should look and think more widely:

- Are there any trees or plants that may provide you with sources of food, fuel or medicine? Try to scavenge textbooks on plants and herbs so that you can begin to develop your skills in spotting useful wild resources.
- What shops are there in your immediate vicinity and what useful things can they provide you with? If you're lucky enough to find a camping goods store, a bookshop, a pharmacy and an unlooted supermarket, of course you're in luck! But even a fashion or jewellery shop can provide sources of useful bedding materials or metals that can be fashioned into tools. Think laterally.
- What homes are there that remain unlooted? Go through the contents in a methodical fashion, room by room – having first ascertained that the previous owners aren't waiting for you in zombie form! – and assess all the available resources.
- If you have to flee your home for any reason, which of the buildings in your area would provide the best shelter? Assess them carefully on your daily walks, and decide on a backup plan for your survival – you may even decide that one of the buildings you discover has advantages compelling enough for you to want to move your base camp.

You may also find that some buildings have already been marked up in spray paint with codes that may be unfamiliar to you. An informal 'zobo code' has developed, and is now used by many survivors to mark up buildings so that they can be easily identified, even from a distance. If you make these marks, ensure that you make them as large as you can and on every side of the building that you can reach. Consult the chart we've provided to decipher any marks you find, but remember that the situation within the building may have changed since the last survivor passed by, and you should proceed with caution even if the code suggests the area is safe.

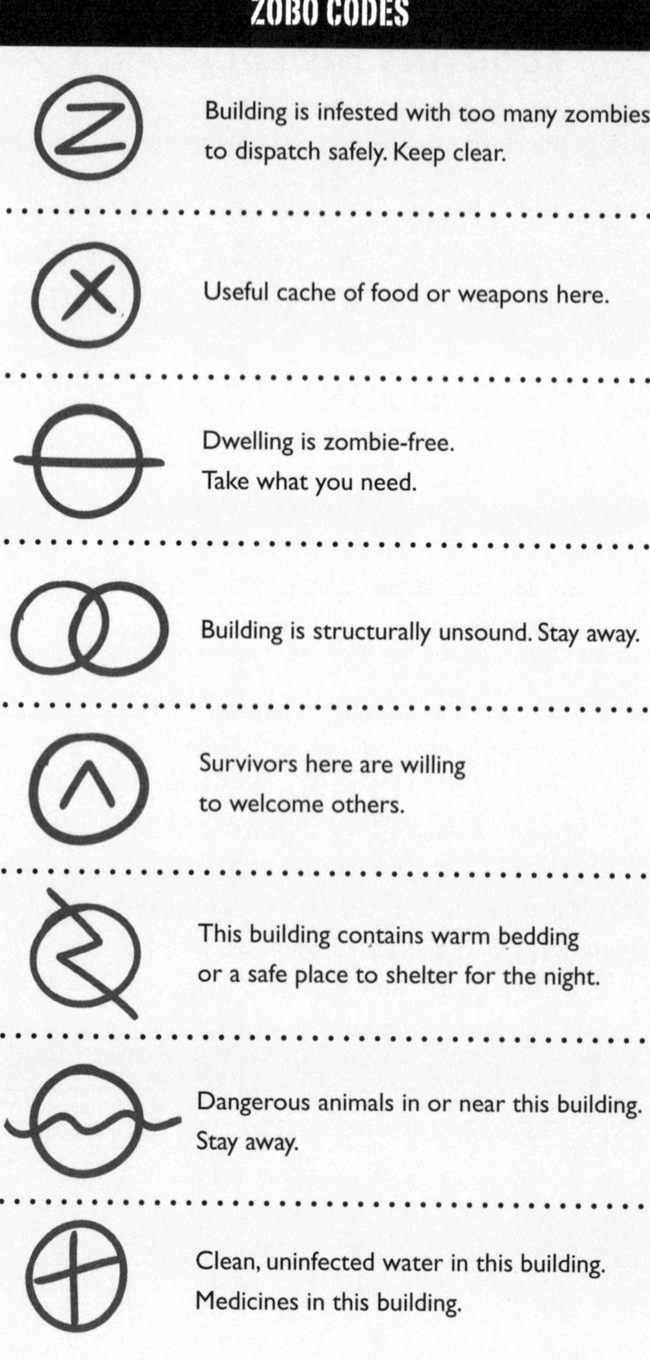

ZOBO CODES
Building is infested with too many zombies to dispatch safely. Keep clear.
Useful cache of food or weapons here.
Dwelling is zombie-free. Take what you need.
Building is structurally unsound. Stay away.
Survivors here are willing to welcome others.
This building contains warm bedding or a safe place to shelter for the night.
Dangerous animals in or near this building. Stay away.
Clean, uninfected water in this building. Medicines in this building.

SCOUTING THE LOCAL AREA: WHAT TO TAKE WITH YOU

On page 155, we discuss how to train yourself to run with a full backpack. Until you've reached this level of fitness, however, you should limit the amount you carry with you so that it won't impede your progress or make it harder for you to escape in the event of zombie attack.

These items are must-carries, however, and you must accustom yourself to walking with the weight of them in your backpack.

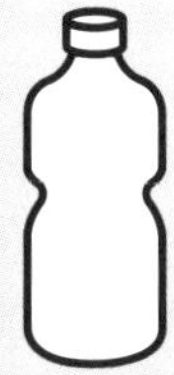

Water. You may be walking for several hours and find only contaminated water. Prioritize water in your scavenging, unless you have a well or stream near your dwelling. Do not risk becoming lightheaded and over-exhausted through dehydration.

A small, light snack – you don't want to eat a full meal while out on reconnaissance. Fruit, cheese, a boiled egg, jerky or crackers are all suitable.

A hat and mittens if it is cold, sunhat or visor if it is warm and sunny. You are best placed to judge whether these things are necessary, but it would be foolish to compromise your fitness for fight or flight.

Binoculars, if you have them, and a map. Take regular sightings to ensure that no zombies are approaching. Mark on the map any areas of interest you might want to return to, or anything unusual you notice.

A handheld torch. You will probably be breaking into dark buildings and will need a source of light to keep you safe, as well as to identify useful supplies.

A weapon, preferably light and handheld. An axe is perfect for this purpose, as you can also use it to break into locked buildings. One of the homemade weapons detailed on page 114 may also prove useful.

You may also like to experiment with walking poles. Some survivors find they are useful for maintaining a good pace on difficult terrain, and they have the added advantage of providing a rudimentary weapon in case of attack.

WALKING SAFELY

You should expect to walk for two to three hours a day to adequately cover your nearby terrain and keep yourself and your home safe, as well as scouting for supplies. However, if you've been cooped up indoors for a long time during a siege, don't expect to be able to walk for three hours on your first day out! If you overdo it, you may end up stiff and sore and have to spend a week recovering – which is of little use in your battle for survival.

We recommend that on the first day you walk briskly for 15–20 minutes, and if that seems to be fairly easy, add another five minutes to your daily walk every few days until you are able to walk for at least an hour continuously. Don't get so out of breath that you couldn't hold a conversation as you walk.

Even an activity as apparently simple and easy on the body as walking can tax the muscles. Make sure that you stretch out thoroughly when you return home from a walk (see page 35) to stop them getting sore.

Find the sturdiest and most comfortable shoes you can. Do not attempt to do your regular walks in high heels, flimsy sandals or fashion shoes. A crawler can be lurking in debris on the road at any point, and the bite from its jaws will be just as deadly as one from the yawning maw of a freshly turned zom.

You may be tempted to listen to an audiobook or podcast – if you are lucky enough to still have the equipment to play such things! – while you're walking. This is not a terrible idea, especially if they will teach you valuable survival techniques or simply take your mind off the horrors your eyes are witnessing. However, only put one headphone on or earbud in at a time – sound is a valuable early warning signal that you are nearing a crowd of zombies. Don't deny yourself this vital advantage.

To step well and improve your stride, be sure that each step rolls from the back of your heel through to push off with your toes. You may be surprised at how much faster and more comfortably you can walk if you spend a little time consciously focusing on your stride.

If you are concerned that you may have flat feet or fallen arches, you might try to raid a shoe shop for orthotic foot supports. Of course, the best plan would be to consult a podiatrist or chiropodist, if you are lucky enough to have access to one!

WHY LEARN TO RUN?

Before the apocalypse, you may have felt that running was not for you. You may have no ambitions to run a marathon, or to experience the 'runner's high'. You may be overweight and believe that running is only for the super-fit.

It is true that if you have significant joint problems, running may not be right for you, and you should try to find a surviving medical professional to consult before embarking on a training regime.

However, remember that the ability to sprint even a few hundred yards has saved lives. Zombies are not, in general, speedy. Their joints have stiffened, their flesh is bloated, their vital fluids leak from them at every step. They find it hard to tackle ladders or even staircases; they often cannot grip a door handle to open it. To escape from a zombie, all you need, in most cases, is to be able to put on a turn of speed so that you can put one of these barriers between you and the zombie chasing you and then dispatch it from a safe distance.

Your major outdoor exercise may always be walking, but if you include a few regular short runs of a minute or two, your body will be ready to run when you are in danger.

And the ability to run for longer distances will be useful to you and to other survivors. The human animal does not have many natural advantages compared to other apex predators; however, we have evolved with endurance-running abilities that are unique among all other primates. It's been theorized that endurance running – that is, the ability to keep on running for very long distances at lowish speeds – was one of the primary factors in our success as a species. And although you might feel that the dominance of the human species is now at an end, the ability to run remains a significant advantage to us.

Running is a very quiet form of transport that needs no special equipment other than a pair of shoes. Running, you are agile and able to take note of your surroundings. You will be able to spot vital supplies in the areas you're running through and collect them, as well as assisting other survivors. Any community will welcome a strong and able runner as a valuable asset.

BEGINNING TO RUN: A PLAN FOR GETTING STARTED, AND HOW TO IMPROVE

- Begin by asking a friend to watch you running over a flat distance – having first of all scouted the area for zombies, naturally! Ask your friend to stand behind you as you run slowly away from them and to watch your feet. Do they roll in slightly, or roll out? If that's the case, you'll need to scavenge shoes that offer more support. Feet that roll inward are 'pronating' – shoes that give support for over-pronation or under-pronation will be labelled as such in a running shoe shop. Or if you happen to have access to a shoe expert, ask for their help and advice!

- Put on some appropriate clothing – something fairly close-fitting, but not too tight, and comfortable. Nothing with dangling straps or belts that could become tangled, and no loose garments that a zombie would find easy to grab.

- Make sure you know your route (see the instructions on picking a safe area in the next section, and those on quartering on page 59).

- For the first eight weeks, run three times a week. Identify a loop that you can cover at a fast walk in ten minutes or so. Begin by walking as fast as you can for half an hour, and include five short periods of slow running – around 30 seconds – spaced evenly during the walk. Each week, increase your jogging time by ten seconds, and add two extra running periods. By the end of the eighth week, you should be able to run for 30 minutes without stopping – although remember that even if you need some breaks, the ability to run will still be useful to you!

- Once you can run for 30 minutes or so, increase the number of times you run to four per week. For two of these four runs, aim to cover at least 4 kilometres, slowly increasing this by 250–500 metres a week. When you can cover seven or eight kilometres fairly easily, we recommend combining your biweekly 'long run' with running errands (see the advice on running with a backpack on page 155).

- To improve further, ensure that one of your biweekly long runs is a hill session. Find a hill which is about 200 metres in length, and see if you can run up and down it ten times.

- Remember not to go too fast – maintain a pace at which you can still breathe comfortably. At the beginning of hill-training, you may well find you need to walk – that is normal. But within a few weeks, you should notice a rapid improvement in your cardiovascular fitness and leg strength.

- Once you can run ten kilometres, turn one of your weekly runs into a speed session. This means doing ten 100-metre flat-out sprints, with at least 90 seconds' recovery time between each 100-metre sprint. If it is possible to do so safely, we recommend that you do these speed-training sessions in an open space such as a park, using markers such as lampposts, park benches or the rudimentary grave markers which litter our public spaces to help your pacing.

BEGINNING TO RUN: DANGERS AND RISKS

Zombies are attracted to human movement. They are predators. They want to eat us. You must not become so engaged in your exercise that you lose focus on the essentials: you won't get anywhere as a runner if you get bitten and turn into one of the living dead.

Observe sensible precautions. Don't try to progress too quickly and listen to your body when you exercise. Notice when you become breathless or get a stitch – in this case, slow down, stretch out and take deeper breaths. Stop at once if you feel any other pain. If possible, try to practise your running in an area which has been cleared of zombies and fenced off. Or get someone in your community to monitor the area while you practise, preferably a sniper or archer, ready to shoot any of the undead that may threaten you.

CASE STUDY

Remember the story of Ms VP of Penrith, who tells us: 'After the apocalypse I was desperate to get fit and healthy. I'd seen so many people chased down and eaten by zoms that I knew I couldn't carry on with my pre-apocalypse ways. If there's anything that'll make you want to start exercising, it's seeing slower people get caught and eaten!

'So, as soon as I could, I started a running routine. Me and my friends were holed up in the primary school down the road from our houses – it had a high fence around it, and a big garden. But after a few weeks I thought it'd be OK to try running up and down the road outside – we hadn't seen any zoms for a few days.

'More fool me! As soon as I started doing some knee-lifts to build muscle, these three massive zombie builders started walking towards me off a building site! I thought it'd be easy to get away, but when I tried to run I pulled a muscle in my foot. I was screaming as I limped down the road away from them! I thought I was dead for sure, I just couldn't run! In the end I was so lucky – my friend heard me and came out and beat the builders with a spade until I got inside our fence.

'Always make sure wherever you're exercising is really 100 per cent zombie-free!'

RUNNING RECORD			
DATE	Distance	Pace	Notes

RUNNING RECORD			
DATE	Distance	Pace	Notes

CYCLING: WHY IT'S A GOOD IDEA, AND WHEN TO AVOID IT

There's no doubt that a working and well-maintained bicycle is a boon to any survival effort, for an individual or for a community. If you have access to a bicycle and the means to keep it maintained, use it as often as you can. But be aware that there are limitations and dangers to using your bicycle in the zombie apocalypse.

- You will be able to move much faster than you can on foot, meaning that you can cover more ground in search of supplies and escape most shambling hordes with ease on roads.
- Bicycle panniers or a basket plus a backpack will enable you to carry more back to your shelter than you can when running.

- The bicycle is almost as silent as a runner – more silent on some surfaces. Unlike when using motorized transport, you will not alert a horde to your presence.

IF THE AREA IN WHICH YOU HAVE MADE YOUR SETTLEMENT IS WELL SUPPLIED WITH GOOD ROADS, A BICYCLE WILL BE A VALUABLE ADDITION TO YOUR SURVIVAL PLANS.

However, be aware of the risks:

- Bicycles are less useful on rough terrain – though skilful riders may avoid these dangers, many may find off-road riding too challenging to be useful.
- A bicycle will not help you to make a quick escape from a horde by, for example, climbing on to the roof of a building. Your natural instinct to stick with your usual mode of transport may hamper you in some circumstances.
- Because it's possible to travel much further on a bike than on foot, you should guard against leaving yourself too far to cycle home before nightfall. Always avoid being out at night, even on a bike, but if you absolutely must ride at night, do use lights.
- Falling off a bicycle at high speed is likely to produce more severe injuries than tripping while running – if you have access to a helmet, wear it. We suggest that bicycle recce missions should ideally consist of at least three people. If one has an accident, the second can go for help while the third waits with the injured person to fight off the living dead should they threaten to attack.

There is one further danger: you may find that you become attached to your bicycle and are unwilling to abandon it when threatened.

CASE STUDY

Consider the case of Ms A-N, who fled Calais through the Channel Tunnel, a journey she likens to a 'hellscape'. Ms A-N says: 'Me and my friend C were on a cycling holiday in Normandy. When everything went crazy, we thought we'd just bike home. We were both great cyclists, we were doing 60, 70 miles a day easy. The Channel Tunnel was the worst. All the passengers on the commuter train had gone zom and broken through the windows. They were clawing at us as we cycled through. At one point, C got a puncture. The zoms were slow, and a bit behind us. She tried to repair the puncture. I kept telling her we had to go, but she loved that bike so much. She called it Bertie. We just didn't have time. I offered her my bike, said I'd run behind. She could have made it if she'd just run. But she wouldn't leave Bertie. So she died. She's probably still in that tunnel.'

Willingness to abandon anything you have picked up if attacked by zombies is vital for your survival. Use your bicycle by all means, but never become attached to it as you might to a living person or animal.

CYCLING: SETTING UP A TRAINING REGIME

This book is not the appropriate place to offer advice on learning to ride a bicycle. In fact, if you have never learned to ride, we strongly suggest that the zombie apocalypse is not the right moment to start! You may think differently if you have access to a paved or tarmacked area which is definitely secure from attack. If you also have a helmet and knee-guards, and a friend to help you learn, by all means begin from scratch.

If you are already a fairly confident rider, you should use a similar strategy to that recommended for training in running. Begin by riding your bike for 30 minutes or so three times a week, noting how much distance you can cover. Then start to increase your riding time by just a few minutes a week. When you can comfortably ride for an hour, add in an extra weekly ride.

Use one of those bicycle rides as 'distance training'; this long ride could eventually cover 50 miles, making you a valuable asset to many townships for long-range scouting and trading with other encampments. Practise riding with baskets and backpack full of heavy equipment so that you will be ready for this.

Use another of your weekly rides as 'hill-training', taking your bike first up gentle hills and then up increasingly steep ones.

THE ABILITY TO ESCAPE QUICKLY UPHILL MAY SAVE YOUR LIFE ONE DAY.

CASE STUDY

Ms SP of Norwich tells us: 'I was never a particularly strong cyclist, but I loved my trusty Brompton in the time before, and I knew it'd be useful even now. I'm lucky that I live in a fairly flat part of the world – perfect for bikes! I ended up in the St Benedict's enclave; those church walls are solid as anything! I'm really proud of the role I have in the community now. I don't have a green finger on either of my hands, I can't cook and I'm as likely to stab myself with a weapon as a zombie – but I can get anywhere within 30 miles of here and back safely. I've traded books and luxury food from the city for medicine and staple foods from the farms near here. I've taken kerosene heaters to people who were stuck in cold, dark places and brought news and gossip all over Norfolk. I've even delivered a baby! I think it makes everyone feel better to know that there are still people who can get around, that we're not all stuck in our little enclaves. I feel like I'm one of the people who's holding the community together.'

CYCLING TIMETABLE

DATE	Mon	Tues	Weds	Thurs	Fri	Sat	Sun

OUTDOOR SWIMMING: WHEN IT MIGHT BE USEFUL, AND WHEN TO AVOID IT

There will be some circumstances in which outdoor swimming is a useful travel method. A lake or river can be a good barrier to zombie attack. The zombies will continue to walk underwater to attack you, but if you can take shelter on an island or manmade structure in the water, the sides will often be too steep for them to climb up. A rowing boat is the ideal way to reach such shelter, but boats are not always available.

In addition, zombies find navigating waterways more difficult than living humans do. To the knowledge of the Ministry, no zombie has ever been observed to swim. Thus, if there is a safe hiding place that can only be reached by swimming – for example, along a deep canal with no towpath – it is likely to be extremely secure.

You may also be able to gather valuable foodstuffs by swimming, either in rivers or lakes or in the ocean. Seaweeds and crustaceans are often best gathered by swimming. And let's not underestimate the pleasure of swimming! For many of us, a swim in the sea is the closest we'll get to a clean bath.

Be aware of the following dangers:

- Pay careful attention to tides in any body of water with which you are unfamiliar – the dangers of riptides haven't gone away just because of the zombie apocalypse. If in doubt, have two friends spot you when you first try swimming in an unfamiliar place, ready to help you if you get into trouble. Make sure you have pre-agreed a signal to use if you need assistance.
- Chunks of zombie flesh can continue to be infectious and we have seen some evidence that the infection can be transmitted through water from recently dead zombies.
- If there are zombies in the water, do not swim unless you have no other option for survival.
- If you see corpses floating face down in the water, gently tap them with a long piece of wood or throw something at them. Make sure they do not move. If they are simply corpses, fish them out and allow time for the water to refresh before you swim.

VENTURING FORTH

OUTDOOR SWIMMING: SETTING UP A TRAINING REGIME

Rather as with cycling, the zombie apocalypse is no time to start learning to swim! Unless you live near a clean, safe body of water whose bottom has been dredged for zombies, you should not be thrashing around looking like an easy meal on the surface of the water as you try to master breaststroke.

However, if you are already a fairly adept swimmer and you have a safe body of water to practise in, you can begin to improve your skills.

- Begin, as in all training, by timing a challenging yet reasonable distance. Perhaps 20 minutes of swimming, 10 times to and from the nearest buoy or some such challenge.
- Then slowly increase the level of difficulty. If you're able to time yourself while swimming, challenge yourself to do the same distance faster.
- Aim to swim three or four times a week for 30-60 minutes per session.
- Increase the number of times you swim to the buoy or the number of minutes you swim for in small increments, perhaps an extra five minutes every week.
- Try to focus on form, making your movements as streamlined as possible: there is no need for you to make any splashing – a splash is lost kinetic energy. Ensure that your strokes aren't straining your neck or back.
- Practise staying underwater for longer periods of time – be careful with this! It would be silly to survive the zombie apocalypse only to succumb to drowning. You may like to time how long you can hold your breath for, and try to increase that time by a second or two every week. But of course it is better to practise this while swimming, so that your body can learn to keep moving while you hold your breath. This skill may be very useful in retrieving underwater objects or in exploring wrecks.

VISITING LONDON AND OTHER BIG CITIES: THE TEMPTATIONS, AND WHY TO STAY AWAY

You may not have the option to stay away from big cities; you may have started your apocalypse in one! If so, you will know all about the risks and dangers of a large urban agglomeration.

However, if you were fortunate enough to begin your apocalypse in a smaller community – a small town, a village, an isolated castle in the Highlands of Scotland – you may be used to thinking of cities as bountiful environments, which you would often visit to acquire the stuff of life. You may be sick of eating boiled barley at every meal and remember fondly the days when you could just drive into the city to pick up food treats, books, new clothes and so on. You will remember our cities as vibrant and lively places.

This is, sadly, no longer the case.

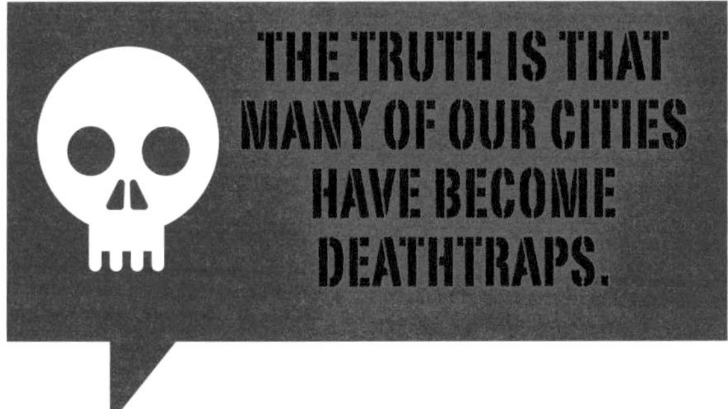

THE TRUTH IS THAT MANY OF OUR CITIES HAVE BECOME DEATHTRAPS.

The main reason for this is, of course, the sheer numbers of the undead. The more living inhabitants there were, the more zombies there are now. Many people in cities lived very close together; it was easy for the virus to spread on packed commuter trains, buses and in particular on the London Underground – there are still tube trains filled with the living dead waiting between stations. No one has had either the time or resources to clean out many of the deadliest areas. Those people who have ended up making their post-apocalypse homes in large cities are well aware of which roads and buildings are safe and which are terrifying hell-houses of horror. But for a visitor, it will be all too easy to make a mistake.

Urban environments are also the least easy to assess for risk. There are no wide vistas across which you can take a sighting of the zombie mass and decide on a strategy of evasion. The next turn around a building may bring you face to face with a horde intent on tearing you limb from limb. In addition, there is the risk of subsidence and the collapse of one or more of the very tall buildings. In at least three places in London that we know of, some system of supports that was carefully braced before the apocalypse has been destroyed and large sinkholes have opened up under buildings or along thoroughfares.

We hope we have adequately explained why 'a quick trip into town' is no longer the pleasant outing it once was! However, we are aware that there may be good reasons why you simply cannot avoid a trip into a city; principle among these, of course, is the search for loved ones.

If you must visit a major city, do not do so alone; preferably go in a group of at least five people, all well-armed, and if possible including a doctor.

Do not under any circumstances travel after dark: aim to camp in a secure location within walking distance of the city and arrive in the city as soon after dawn as you can. And take advantage of any and all intelligence available on what may face you inside the city. If there are maps, use them. If you can contact someone on ROFFLENET who can advise you of the danger zones, ask all your questions.

VISITING LONDON: AN ANALYSIS

Visiting London without an up-to-date map and preferably a knowledgeable and seasoned guide is exceedingly ill advised. The city's zombie horde distribution changes day by day, and even the fairly reliable landmarks we refer to here might have to be abandoned in case of substantial incursion. Don't put your life at risk by relying on an old guide.

Having said that, if you are in London unexpectedly and need to find shelter quickly, here are some pointers which are likely to remain valid:

Buckingham Palace is and has been protected from zombie incursion by His Majesty's guards since shortly after the outbreak. If in danger, citizens may take shelter in the palace, although strict quarantine regulations are in place. Readers will be aware that a great number of the Royal Family tragically perished and are unlikely to be seen at the Palace except in zombie form.

Regent's Park has been turned into farmland and is maintained by a team of Ministry volunteers. A secure perimeter has been erected and the 'safe zone' between **Regent's Park**, the **British Library**, **Broadcasting House** and the **British Museum** is generally fairly peaceful and should be your first port of call should you find yourself stranded in London or if you have travelled here to find loved ones.

The Ministry itself is now housed in Broadcasting House and the neighbouring Langham Hotel. We are six to a room, so it can be a tight squeeze if you're used to more generous arrangements in the countryside, but we will provide for any living person in need of assistance.

The London Eye is infested with zombies in every pod and should be considered extremely hazardous. It has occasionally been known for a zombie to smash through the glass and drop down on to a passer-by.

The Gospel Oak area is rumoured to be home to a team of expert zombie-killers who may offer shelter to travellers in an emergency.

Whitehall and **Westminster Abbey** are unfortunately lost to the zombies at present.

The National Gallery is slowly being emptied of its treasures, which we are relocating to Broadcasting House. If you have any expertise in art curation, restoration or upkeep we would be delighted to hear from you and can offer you the chance to work with an unparalleled collection.

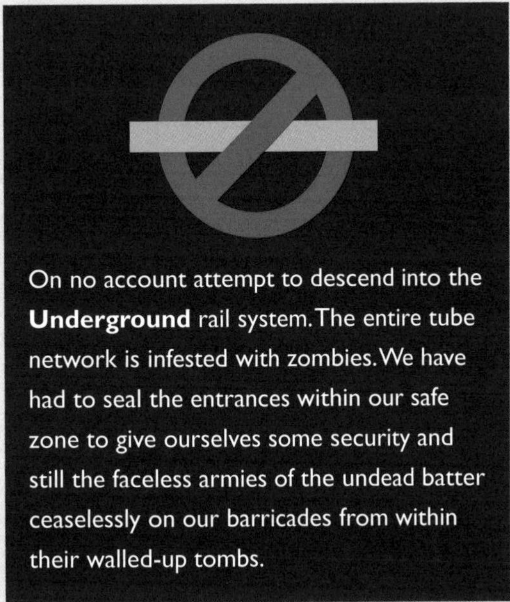

On no account attempt to descend into the **Underground** rail system. The entire tube network is infested with zombies. We have had to seal the entrances within our safe zone to give ourselves some security and still the faceless armies of the undead batter ceaselessly on our barricades from within their walled-up tombs.

CASE STUDY: Maxine Myers

I spent the early apocalypse working 18-hour shifts in A&E – I'm a doctor, but we ended up calling in anyone who had medical experience to help out with the 'flu' sufferers arriving for treatment. It took us too long to realize we had nothing to offer. I'm ashamed when I think of the bad advice I gave, of the people I sent home to infect their loved ones. There's nothing I can do about that now, but I think about it all the time.

Once we realized we were looking at a pathogen like no other we'd ever encountered, a few of us barricaded ourselves inside the hospital, trying to get some answers and keeping some of our patients alive. We survived for a few weeks on the food from the canteen storeroom and distilled water. But we were idiots to think we could save any of our patients. All we could do in the end was give them a merciful death.

After ... I guess it must've been three or four weeks, we sat down and discussed what to do. There were four of us left by that time. We decided that we owed it to anyone left alive to try to find them, to help if we could. To give medical advice and teach other people what we knew. At least to share what we'd learned about the virus. The paramedic wanted to look for her parents, in the south. The other doctor was going south too, so they travelled together. I was looking for my partner, Paula, who I hadn't heard from since the outbreak and Rick, an ambulance guy, was heading in the same direction.

As soon as we opened up our barricaded doors and heard the silence – remember when that silence seemed so new and eerie? – we realized that we'd need to be well supplied before we tried to get out of town. Rick and I grabbed two bikes and started scouting the area, covering miles and miles every day, looking for other survivors, picking up supplies from camping and army surplus stores. Bikes were great because the roads were well maintained and empty; and we found 'zobo code' intel on the walls which saved our skins a couple of times.

We planned our routes meticulously. Got maps, drew a plan A, plan B, plan C. Ever since the start of the apocalypse, it's helped me to keep focused on what needs to be done next. I've never been very interested in looking back – learn from the past, but then just keep trucking. As long as you're alive, there's hope, and something good might be coming along tomorrow.

VENTURING FORTH

Rick and I got separated as we left the city. We just got split up by a horde coming out of a collapsing building. We were heading in the same direction so I always thought we'd find each other again but we never did. I hope he's OK. We hadn't really spoken before the apocalypse, but he was a good friend. If he's out there somewhere, I hope he reads this and gets in touch. And if not ... I'll always remember him. Sometimes that's all you can give people.

NOTES

SECTION 03

BUILDING A COMMUNITY

BUILDING A COMMUNITY

INTRODUCTORY REMARKS

You have survived your first siege, or perhaps a succession of sieges, each debilitating in its own way. You have ventured out into the changed landscape and have become very familiar with your new environment. Alone, or perhaps with a small group, you have picked a safe place to live, set up your defences and begun to become proficient in travelling and scavenging.

Why, you may ask, risk all this by deliberately attempting to make contact with other survivors? You may have heard stories, on ROFFLENET or passed by word of mouth, of human beings who have sunk immediately to savagery and brutality, of serial killers who are taking advantage of the current mayhem to practise their evil arts, of communities that have wholeheartedly embraced cannibalism or torture. It is very surprising how many urban legends there are regarding cannibalism, as if this were a latent desire in all humanity which has only needed this unrest to manifest itself!

Rest assured: among the survivors there is likely to be no higher a proportion of cannibals, murderers and sadists than there was among the general population in the time before. Certainly, dangerous people exist and you must take precautions. But one is as likely to have survived this apocalypse by the virtues of patience, hard work, loyalty and courage as by a liking for brutality and killing. Perhaps more likely: escaping a zombie horde, constructing well-made defences or hiding tend to be better strategies than running towards them yelling with bloodlust. (See the 'Essentials of zombie-fighting' section on page 112.)

It follows that in your immediate environment there are likely to be a number of people like you: afraid, alone, uncertain and yet basically decent. They are also likely to be craving human companionship and the benefits of being part of a group working together. They may be odd. They may not have been your 'kind of person' in the time before. But we are all each other's kind of people now. The living are our kind of people.

There are many advantages of working together in a larger group. There are economies of scale in food gathering, growing and preparation. You are more likely to encounter useful specialists with knowledge of how to set up, for example, electricity or communications networks, or how to make waterproof clothing or customize bicycles. The progress of humanity throughout the millennia has been directly proportional to the number of humans in the world: we are weak alone; it is our capacity to work together that makes us strong.

BUILDING A COMMUNITY

GETTING STARTED: MAKING CONTACT WITH OTHER SURVIVORS IN YOUR AREA

- Your daily walks are likely to be of use to you here. You may encounter signs of life, or even another person out for a walk. Talk to them; use your instincts to gauge how likely or unlikely their stories are to be true. Do not immediately accept an invitation to visit their home – unless you're under attack! – but begin with friendly greetings and perhaps exchanging gifts. You will begin to get a sense of who you can trust and who you can't.

- You may want to put up a flier, or a message on ROFFLENET, suggesting that any people in your neighbourhood gather together on a particular day to take part in a communal project. You may know, for example, that there's a large reservoir of fresh water in a building whose entrance is currently covered by fallen trees. This would be an example of a communal project which no one would be able to tackle individually but which would benefit everyone. These kinds of project will foster trust and encourage people to see the benefits of working together.

- We have heard of survivors who have brought a community together by playing music or singing together at the same time every day or week. Now that the world is so quiet, music carries across long distances and is an instant indicator that there are living humans having fun – an attractive proposition! However, you must be conscious of the danger of attracting zombies as well as friends. By all means put on an entertainment event semi-regularly if you can, but make sure that you do so safely.

- Offer to help people in your area who seem to be vulnerable or in need of help. A parent with small children may be grateful for a regular canned goods run; a person trapped indoors by a disability or infirmity may have survived relatively easily, being used to staying safe inside, but may be grateful for more books or other entertainment media.

- Remember that you yourself are also a stranger, of whom others may be wary. You will have to build up trust in each other.

- Setting up a project in a public area in which others can participate without having to meet each other may also be a way to build trust. For example: setting up a communal garden by clearing flower beds and planting your own seeds may encourage other survivors to add their seeds to the common wealth.

WORKING TOGETHER: SETTING UP A COMMUNAL KITCHEN

One of the most tried-and-tested ways to encourage a community to begin to work together is to set up a communal kitchen. In fact, this endeavour is so important – and so welcoming – that it deserves to be discussed in some detail.

The benefits need little spelling out. By combining food resources, you are likely to achieve a more balanced diet with greater nutritional variety than by simply hoarding your own jerky or tinned butter beans and eating them alone. By using everyone's skills and abilities, you'll be able to harvest, hunt or scavenge more food (see page 167 on food-gathering). You'll be able to take advantage of the skills of the best cooks. And, perhaps most importantly, you'll be able to settle down to a communal meal several times a week; it's simply pleasant to eat in company, it is a peaceful way to end the day, and one which reminds us of happier times and of our shared humanity.

Since our ancestors' hunter-gatherer days, gathering around the campfire to eat roasted meat has been a sign of plenty and ease. There is a reason why many religious groups – monasteries, convents or retreats – insist that every member of the group works together in the communal kitchen. There is a calm and collegiate feeling to be found in creating a meal together.

You might like to begin by suggesting a safe and secure place for a communal meal. Perhaps it is your own shelter. Perhaps there is a large building standing derelict that has a long dining room or large kitchen; maybe a school, an office building with a cafeteria, or a restaurant. We have heard of survivors who gather four times a week to cook a meal together in the kitchens of an abandoned railway station, eating the food in the waiting rooms on the platform!

There is no need for the meal to be elaborate. Encourage everyone to bring what they can, around two hours before you intend to eat. The most experienced cook in your group should regard this kind of cooking – combining what there is into a sumptuous meal – as a great challenge. If you are organizing the event, you might like to make sure that some staples are provided: for example, a bag of rice, clean water and a bottle of oil (see the next section on suggested meals).

Paper plates or plastic cutlery have no role in these times. You might ask each participant to bring their own bowl, spoon, fork and mug. That way, if you cannot provide the facilities to wash up, everyone will have only one set of utensils to rinse themselves when they get home.

SAMPLE MEALS – TO BE STRETCHED WITH WHATEVER YOU HAVE

This kind of cooking has been the basis of 'peasant food' since time immemorial: simple, rustic meals that are designed to be improved with whatever you have available. It is helpful if the host can provide the first two or three ingredients, with the remainder of the ingredients being whatever is to hand or is contributed by the rest of the group. These ad hoc ingredients can be incorporated in various ways.

MIXED INGREDIENT RISOTTO

Host to supply: bag of rice, clean water, bottle of oil

Fry the rice and other flavoursome ingredients for a few minutes until the rice is slightly toasted and golden. Add water – three times the volume of the rice – bring to a boil and cook for 20–30 minutes, along with any protein you want to add to the meal. Add other ingredients towards the end of the cooking time.

'Other ingredients' for this recipe are almost limitless. The 'flavoursome ingredients' added at the start of the cooking process might include onions, garlic, pungent herbs and spices. Once the water is added, you can include almost any protein, for example: fish (ensuring all bones have been removed), chicken, beef, lamb, pork or sausage. You could also add hard vegetables like carrots, broccoli, parsnips or cauliflower. Towards the end of the process, to cook for just five or ten minutes, you can add softer vegetables such as peas, green leafy vegetables like spinach, and you could even crack some eggs on to the top of the dish to cook for the last few minutes.

SIMPLE STEW

Host to supply: protein (meat or pulses), oil and water

Begin by frying meat, if you have some, with some onion, garlic or leeks for five to ten minutes, until you see some brown caramelization on the meat and vegetables. Then add any other vegetables you have available, especially root vegetables such as potatoes and carrots, and canned pulses. (If you're using dried pulses, you should soak them overnight, cook them separately in water and bring them to a rapid boil for at least 20 minutes before adding to the stew.) Then add liquid. This could be clean water, wine or beer if you have it, or canned tomatoes. Cook slowly for two hours. If you have the ingredients, you can add dumplings to the top of the stew: make them by combining three parts flour with one part fat and one part water into a sticky dough, rolling it into balls and popping them into the top of the stew for the last 20 minutes of the cooking time.

WORKING TOGETHER: GATHERING SUPPLIES AND HUNTING

Once you are working in a larger community, your first priority should be to streamline your food gathering.

- **Ask all members of your community to describe their expertise from the time before.** This may be difficult; many people do not like to remember the time before, and may be shy of taking on work duties that remind them of their previous lives. You should try to be respectful of this, but if someone in your community has experience in agriculture or food production it may be vital that they use their knowledge to help everyone to survive.

- **Allot community members jobs according to their interests, enthusiasm and experience.** Anyone with previous hunting experience should be put to work in this capacity if possible. Children are often particularly good at gathering wild food – berries and nuts, for example – once they have been shown what they're looking for.

- **Hunting parties should focus on laying traps rather than on active chase-hunting.** For one thing, in most parts of Britain the pickings are thin for hunting. But more importantly, a hunting party tends to be rather loud – even the retort of a rifle can draw zombies. Setting traps and fishing are safer bets by far. You should familiarize yourselves with traps designed to catch squirrels and rabbits (see page 173 on hunting in the Food for Heroes chapter).

- **All members of the community who are able to do so should spend some time every day gathering food,** even if this is only walking a route which is likely to take them near to shops that can be looted. Food-gathering parties should, if possible, consist of at least three people.

- **All food found by members of the community should be shared by the whole community.** We all know from the time before that a community member who is skilled with electrical equations can be as useful as someone who can hunt or fish. It is invidious to allow favouritism in sharing of food, or to practise an 'eat what you kill' policy. If a community member is repeatedly shirking any useful work, see page 101 on 'how to punish infractions'.

- **Remember that food-gathering can be extremely bonding and enjoyable for the group!** This is a set of skills which our ancestors have practised since the evolution of our species. You may be surprised at how natural it feels to work together to lay and check traps or to find the tastiest berries.

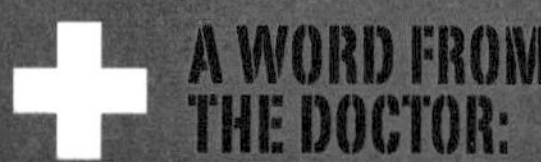

THE CHRONICALLY ILL DURING THE ZOMBIE APOCALYPSE

We have lost so many people: over 90 per cent of the previous population of the United Kingdom is dead or undead. This means that every human life is precious. Even if you are chronically ill – physically or in your mental health – please believe that humanity needs you. In fact, those people who have been used to living very simply, able to accomplish only a few tasks every day, focusing on maintaining a supply of food, shelter and medication, have a lot to teach the rest of us! If you are chronically ill, you have probably already developed survival and mental health strategies that you can helpfully share with your community.

In your case, it will be particularly important to team up with a communal group, who should be able to scavenge for the medications you need and help you with other necessities of life. Whatever the effects of your condition, there are certainly ways you can contribute to your community; we can offer suggestions, but you'll be able to come up with better ideas for yourself!

Constructing traps and snares is a good example of a low-energy but highly important task that chronically ill people may be able to help with during the zombie apocalypse (see page 175). The chronically ill may have the time and energy to peruse books from the time before to seek out useful strategies for survival, or they may find a role as a mediator of disputes (see page 101). Whatever level of energy you have, please know that your contribution is wanted and needed by the people around you!

TASKS ALLOTTED TO COMMUNITY MEMBERS		
Name	**Task**	**Day of week**

SIMPLE WAYS TO WORK TOGETHER: RECREATION NIGHTS

Even if your community is fairly disparate – perhaps spread over a number of crofts in the Highlands of Scotland, or split up between various small safe-houses in a suburban street – and it's impossible to get together most evenings for a meal, you can still arrange periodic recreation nights to foster community cohesion.

You may find that some members of your community have very different ideas about what constitutes a good night out! Some may want to begin home-brewing, whereas others may be teetotal. Some may enjoy endless conversation, while others simply want to be left alone to read, draw or just to think.

If you are the person who is organizing the recreation nights, it is as well to get an idea from each person you're intending to invite of what their interests are. Then you can arrange a series of events which might appeal to – or be run by – different members of your community. Plan the events well in advance so that people who would not enjoy a night reading of Allen Ginsberg's *Howl* will be able to avoid that particular evening's entertainment and plan their own fun.

If you happen to have a working generator and sufficient excess power to work one of the many entertainment formats of the previous age, have at it! However, for most of us, films, television and recorded music are rare treats to be enjoyed communally. We have therefore compiled a list of suggestions for communal recreation nights that can be enjoyed without using any fuel or power.

- **Making music is an ideal communal activity.** Musical instruments can be played without power, singing can be enjoyed even in the dark or by the light of a single candle – the Ministry has heard many reports of people who enjoy quiet nights of song, homemade music and dancing much more than the 'club nights' of the pre-apocalypse days. Learning an instrument is a worthwhile use of one's leisure time; if you are able, holding an old-fashioned ceilidh will both entertain and improve the health of your community.

- **If you lack the capability to enjoy electronic entertainments, why not invent your own low-tech versions of them?** Get together as a community to perform the stories from favourite films and television programmes, including classic British stories such as *Harry Potter* and *Doctor Who*. Invent your own adventures for your favourite superheroes and keep the stories alive.

- **Both reading aloud and being read to can be deeply enjoyable.** This could be combined with a 'book group', in which works of literature are discussed.

- **Experiment with board games, card games and even role-playing games.** If there are no boards or sets of cards where you are, it is relatively easy and fun to design a set of playing cards or create your own chessboard. Many apocalypse survivors have come to enjoy games like Demons and Darkness, which give us some light relief from the horrors of our daily lives.

- **Organize a lecture series.** Each of us had a life in the past in which we were expert in some particular area, or had a hobby which we enjoyed. Encourage each member of your group to give a talk or lead a workshop in a skill which they have knowledge of. In this way you may end up learning basic human biology, the essentials of anthropology or art history, or simply the best way to deal with a bully in the workplace! You'll also get to know one another better, and begin to get a sense of what roles each member of your community may be suited for.

- **Take inspiration from the indigenous peoples of the Arctic and hold a version of 'Inuit Games'** in which you demonstrate your prowess in various zombie-defence tasks, competing to be named champion. The challenges could include: 'head-chopping' a block of wood (which has the benefit of resulting in additional chopped firewood), 'dodge-running' a slalom of angry zombies in the fastest time without being captured, or 'brain-crushing' pumpkins or marrows (remember to cook the smashed vegetables afterwards). We strongly advise against using live zombies, or even zombie corpses, for these contests. It is all too easy for a lump of infected flesh to splatter into an open mouth or eyes. Safety is paramount.

SIMPLE WAYS TO WORK TOGETHER: TEAMING UP TO TRAIN

It can be deeply enjoyable to involve another person – or several people – in your training routine. The companionship and challenge can encourage each person to work harder while having fun. But it can also be demotivating and distressing to see that you are – perhaps – the slowest or least able in the group.

- Perhaps the simplest way to involve other people in your training routine is a simple 'reporting in' function. Tell another person that you intend to train today. Report back to say that you've done it and congratulate each other on a job well done.

- Take part in different activities but in the same area. One person may be doing squats and crunches while another friend does timed sprints and a third completes bicep curls. You can encourage each other, look out for good form, and enjoy one another's company while not being directly in competition.

- If you feel it will not be disheartening for you, by all means complete the same course or activity with friends or other community members who are faster than you are. They may run while you walk, but you can all enjoy the same crisp air, appreciate the autumn leaves and keep a watchful eye out for the living dead together.

- One of the best ways to train together is to practise combat manoeuvres – it is advisable for everyone to know some basic defensive moves against zombie attack, and you will do better if you know the strengths and weaknesses of the people who live alongside you. See page 122 on training together for more information.

IS THERE STILL A ROLE FOR ORGANIZED SPORT?

Team sports have been a part of fitness and entertainment for centuries; for those who enjoy them they're a great way to maintain community spirit as well as improving all sorts of fitness outcomes.

These days, organizing a quick kick-about or a five-a-side netball game is fraught with problems. The most obvious difficulty is noise: the sound of a hard-fought game is likely to attract zombies, especially if there are spectators. Zombies are also particularly drawn to certain body movements – there's some evidence that knee-lifts and high-kicks are especially attractive to them, as they mimic the visual cues of injured prey.

Never attempt to play a ball game or team sport in an area which is not fully secured against zombie incursion. Sports are extremely engrossing and distracting. Even if there are no zombies nearby, players and supporters are likely to be so interested in the match that they simply won't be able to pay full attention to lookout duties.

However, if you have access to a totally secure area – for example, a walled garden or a fenced-off part of a guarded compound – team games can be a great way to blow off steam and keep healthy. Many games can be adapted for smaller team sizes; basketball, netball, football, rugby, baseball and rounders require very few pieces of equipment, and little that is needed for day-to-day defence.

If there have been squabbles in your settlement or community, team games are a healthy channel for aggression. If you're able to travel safely, why not organize an inter-settlement league? Or you can post the results of your matches on ROFFLENET, with accounts of the matches. Some very fine accounts of cricket matches from a small township near Dulverton in Exmoor have become very popular in recent months. Players could compete for luxury items such as cakes, or pretty but useless objects such as jewels or gold.

In this context, it's worth briefly mentioning that there will often be opportunities to turn a long mission or set of tasks into a game. For example, several townships have set up a leader board in their mess halls for the number of zombies killed or crawlers decapitated – this messy and dull work must be done by someone and a bit of competition can make the whole thing a little less grim. It may seem disrespectful to turn an event as appalling as the zombie apocalypse into a game, but the results speak for themselves and we at the Ministry say: **Whatever gets you through!**

THE PITFALLS OF COMMUNAL LIFE: WHAT TO DO WHEN YOU REALLY ANNOY EACH OTHER

Before the fall of civilization across the world, many of us were able to live in social bubbles. Many people lived alone. If we lived with others, we had chosen those companions ourselves. In wealthier countries, very few of us, as adults, had to share a bedroom with a total stranger – or many total strangers! – with whom we had little in common for months or years. We often had access to a wide variety of media, and could curate what we watched, read and listened to as carefully as we chose our housemates and social activities.

Those days are gone. For most of us, friends and family from the time before are dead. If we are lucky, a partner, friend, child, parent or sibling may have survived. Very few of us are fortunate enough to know more than one or two people with whom we were close in the time before.
In a certain sense, this is a blessing. We are not constantly reminded of the life we have lost. Most of us will have found what we once learned in primary school – that, thrown together with a group of strangers, it is natural to find some companionship. We may not like the same TV shows or support the same football team, but we have the urgent struggle for survival in common and that is enough.

However, it is natural for disagreements to erupt. We are often forced to live together in close quarters, and we do not have many of the distractions we're used to.

CASE STUDY

Mrs V of Hetton-le-Hole, Tyne and Wear, tells us: 'Me and six others survived because we were in the local Spar shop. We worked well together to fight off the zoms – and we managed to barricade ourselves in with all that tinned food. We were there for eight weeks, but some of the others just couldn't get on. There was this teenage boy, Bobby, who'd bicker all the time with an older gent, Vikram. Stupid things. Who'd had the last Shortbread Santa. Whose turn it was to tip the slops bucket off the roof. In the end, Bobby ran off – we all tried to stop him, but he wouldn't listen. The horde eventually moved on ... but we saw Bobby in the pack of zombies. Or what was left of Bobby.'

Don't let this happen to you or your group.

- Set up written rules for the distribution of valuable commodities and treats – decide between yourselves whether equal portions of food are given to all, or whether more food is given to those who have done most physical labour. Decide whether treats are earned or distributed according to a schedule. Vote on your system, write it down and stick to it.
- Appoint a mediator – vote on the member of your group most likely to be able to maintain fairness in a dispute and agree to let them decide the outcome of any quarrel.
- Settle disagreements by the flip of a coin or by a game of chance, like drawing cards or Ludo.
- If your group contains an awkward member – many do – agree a rota for dealing with their difficult behaviour and support one another if they attempt to annoy others or are overly demanding.
- If at all possible, make allowances for the need for solitude and privacy. Setting aside a small corner as a curtained-off 'reading area' can make all the difference.

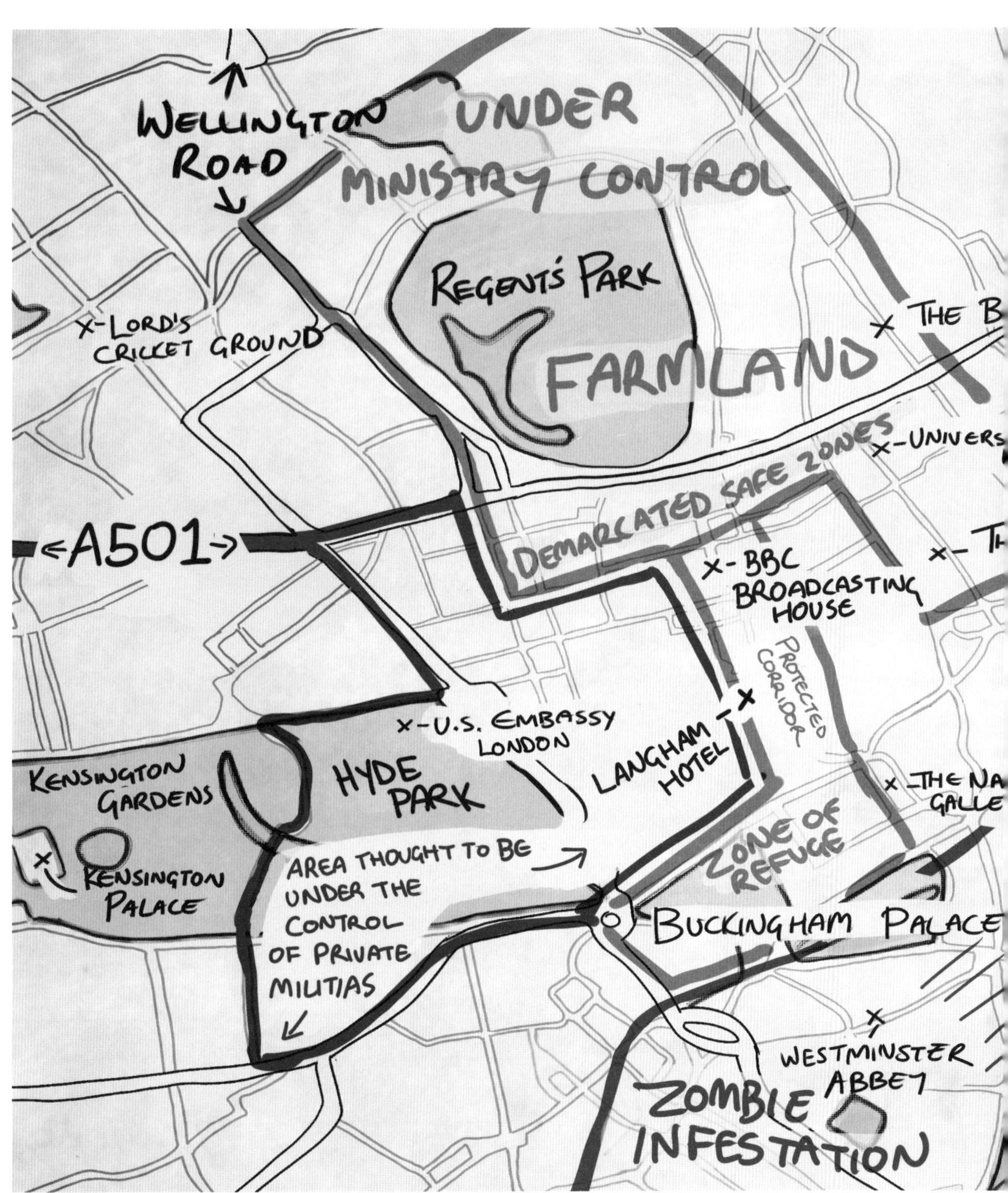

WELLINGTON ROAD
UNDER MINISTRY CONTROL
REGENTS' PARK
FARMLAND
X-LORD'S CRICKET GROUND
X THE B
X-UNIVERS
DEMARCATED SAFE ZONES
<A501>
X-BBC BROADCASTING HOUSE
X-TH
PROTECTED CORRIDOR
X-U.S. EMBASSY LONDON
LANGHAM HOTEL
KENSINGTON GARDENS
HYDE PARK
X-THE NA GALLE
ZONE OF REFUGE
X KENSINGTON PALACE
AREA THOUGHT TO BE UNDER THE CONTROL OF PRIVATE MILITIAS
BUCKINGHAM PALACE
WESTMINSTER ABBEY
ZOMBIE INFESTATION

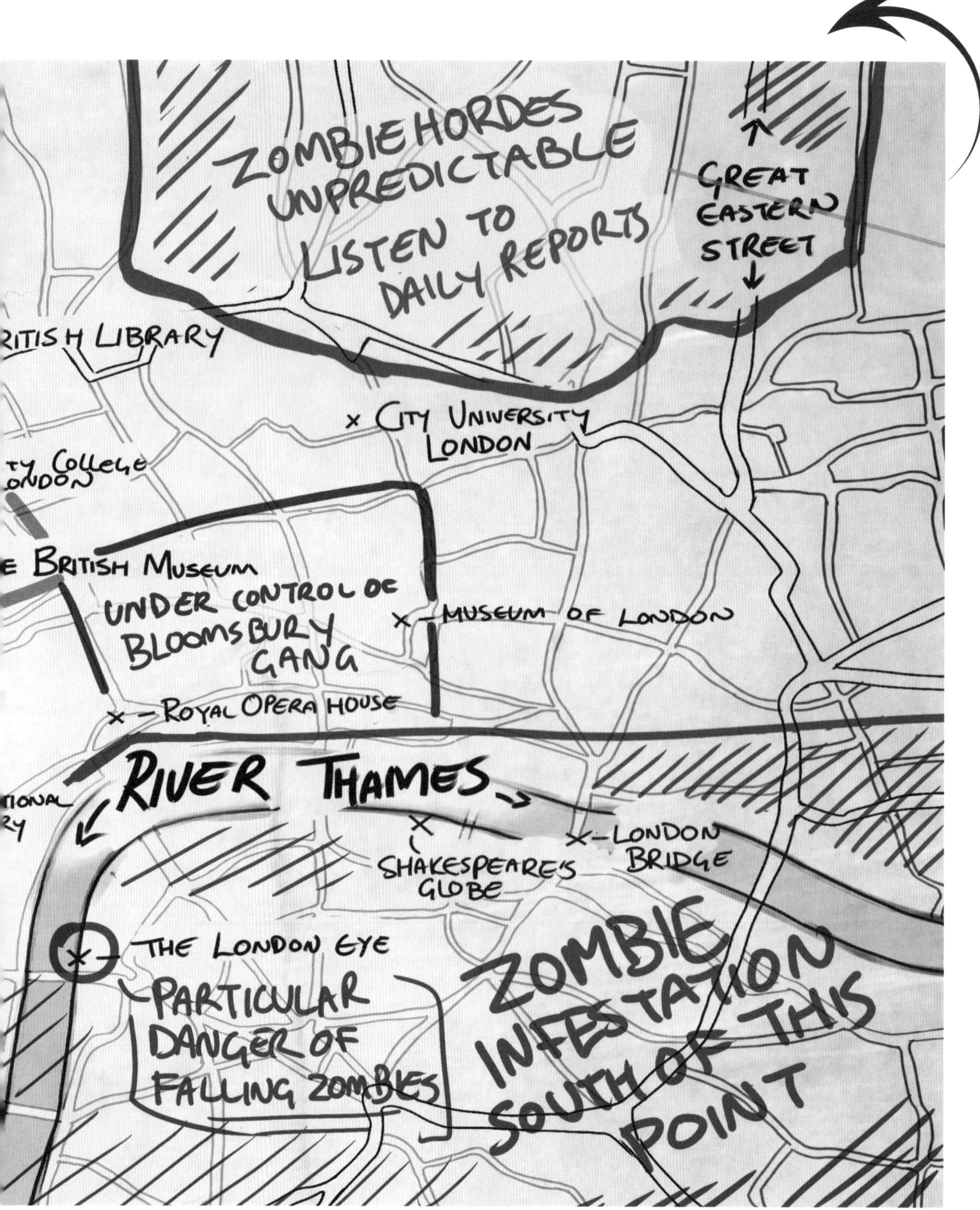
ZOMBIE HORDES UNPREDICTABLE
LISTEN TO DAILY REPORTS
GREAT EASTERN STREET
RITISH LIBRARY
CITY UNIVERSITY LONDON
TY COLLEGE ONDON
E BRITISH MUSEUM
UNDER CONTROL OF BLOOMSBURY GANG
MUSEUM OF LONDON
ROYAL OPERA HOUSE
RIVER THAMES
TIONAL RY
SHAKESPEARE'S GLOBE
LONDON BRIDGE
THE LONDON EYE
PARTICULAR DANGER OF FALLING ZOMBIES
ZOMBIE INFESTATION SOUTH OF THIS POINT

THE PITFALLS OF COMMUNAL LIFE: HOW TO PUNISH INFRACTIONS WHEN THERE'S NO LONGER A WORKING POLICE FORCE OR LEGAL SYSTEM

The punishment of infractions is a complex matter. For minor infractions – stealing, not using the latrine in the agreed way, hoarding resources – minor punishments may be appropriate. For example:

REMOVAL OF TREATS

ONE MISSED MEAL

AN AFTERNOON OF A DISPLEASING WORK DUTY, SUCH AS CLEANING A DIRTY AREA

12 HOURS OF SOLITARY CONFINEMENT – SOLITARY IS A SEVERE PUNISHMENT AND SHOULD ONLY BE USED FOR VERY LIMITED AMOUNTS OF TIME

If you have to deal with a major crime, we encourage you to consult Ministry Briefing no. 191, which contains provisional government regulations. In summary, this paper suggests:

1. If a member of your community is accused of a very serious crime you must hold a trial if at all possible. It is necessary for the life of the community for crimes to be investigated and for criminals to be held to account. Giving up on this principle means giving up on all that makes human life worth fighting for. Even a statement from a witness and a vote by community members is better than summary justice.

2. We encourage communities to attempt to act according to the principles of 'truth and reconciliation'. We do not have enough humans left alive to waste life lightly. Deep conversation over a period of time may convince the group that there is no danger that the crime will occur again.

3. If the member of your community who committed the crime seems very likely to pose a significant danger, if there is no possibility of holding them captive and if all other recourses have been exhausted, the Ministry advice is to record their physical features and post a warning on ROFFLENET, and then to expel them from your community. We understand that this solution is unsatisfactory in many ways. However, it is the most palatable that we have been able to devise.

MAKING TIME FOR REST AND RECREATION

It is too easy to work all the time. The fight for survival is exhausting indeed, and can often feel overwhelming. But if you are not in imminent danger – and if you are organizing a community for long-term survival – you must make time for recreation.

For centuries, many communities around the world took each seventh or eighth day as a rest day, making for four rest days in every cycle of the moon. Rest days are also vital in any health and fitness routine. Even if you are stuck indoors with nothing to do other than counting the faces of the departed pressed against your windows, give your muscles one rest day from strength training every week. You should not give all the people in your community a rest day on the same day – someone must keep a lookout for the shambling gait of the living dead. But arranging times when almost everyone is able to stop working is a good idea.

For some communities, this may mean arranging a communal meal most evenings, when you can catch up with one another and reflect on the day's work. For others, it could be a sewing, knitting, engine-repair, plumbing-skills or weapon-making circle: these skills must be practised and passed on now. Even if we don't need to use them yet, we'll need them in our lifetimes, and working on them communally can be enjoyable and relaxing.

CASE STUDY

DS of Wolverhampton recalls: 'When we were first setting up the Prosser Street enclave, we just worked all day and all night – digging our moats, putting up fortifications, cementing the arms turrets into the Gurdwara. We didn't have time to think about anything but staying alive. But after a few weeks, some people in the community suggested that we could start doing morning meditation. There were a few complaints that it was a waste of time! But the zombies are usually really quiet just about dawn, and it made for a peaceful start to the day. A time to feel like human beings, you know? A lot of us do the meditation now. You don't have to be religious, it's just good for you to have time to just sit and be.'

MAKING TIME FOR CELEBRATION

It may feel to you that there's not a lot to celebrate. Everyone that you love is dead. Your daily life is a relentless battle just to stay alive. We are mocked by the shuffling corpses of those we once called our friends, neighbours, postmen and PE teachers.

But we are alive. That in itself, though it may not feel like much, is everything. If there is a religious or cultural festival that you have enjoyed celebrating in the past, continue with that practice. Remember that Jewish people observed the Jewish festivals in Auschwitz, that fighting stopped on Christmas Day during the First World War. These times have meaning for us that is beyond circumstance. They connect us to our past and allow us to imagine a better tomorrow.

To that end, the Ministry also suggests that your own community should nominate a 'founding day' to be celebrated annually. This could be the day you first came to the place where you all live, or the day when you first cleared the building of zombies. Perhaps in the future this founding day will be remembered by your grandchildren, or their grandchildren. Tell the stories of how you arrived in the place where you live now. Remember how hard it was in those early days. Remember how far you've come and how much has been achieved.

Even if you are a community of one or two, take time to remember your history. Mark other days too. Remember the date of an important victory in the battle over the zombies, or the day when you first harvested crops you'd grown yourselves. Celebrate your own birthdays and those of any children born to the community.

We hope one day to institute 'VZ Day', the day of victory over the zombie plague. We are not there yet, but we will be. Until then, we suggest that communities mark 1 May – a traditional day for a spring festival – as Survival Day. It is a day on which we remember our own survival, when we tell our stories and express our hope for a new spring for humanity.

MAKING TIME FOR MOURNING

The need for mourning has no explanation: most of us will have days marked in the calendar which are specifically significant to us for the loss of loved ones.

We would encourage you to mark these days every year with a day of quiet contemplation. Many people may like to light a candle, visit a special spot if possible, perform acts of service or do things which their loved one might especially have enjoyed. It is a good idea to let those around you know which dates will be particularly hard for you, so that they can prepare to support you.

The Ministry has chosen 22 July as the day we collectively remember the dead of the zombie apocalypse. This was the day of a great battle during which humanity began to fight back against the plague itself rather than individual zombies. We remember our dead on the same day that we remember our struggle: to remind ourselves that even after disaster there will be defiance and hope.

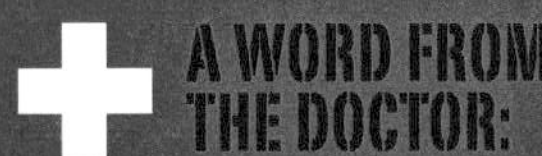

WHAT TO TELL YOUR SURVIVING CHILDREN ABOUT THE ZOMBIE APOCALYPSE

We all wish our children hadn't seen the things they've seen. We try to shield them from the worst of the destruction around us. But we know they've seen more than any child should see. There's no way to come through this unscathed; it's heartbreaking.

However, there are some things you can say to your kids that might make it easier for them:

- 'It's OK to talk about what you've seen' – always make time to listen to a child who wants to talk about a difficult thing they've seen. You can't make it better. But you can listen and agree that it was scary, and, if appropriate, work out together what they should do in a similar scary situation.
- 'It's OK not to talk about it' – children might not want to have these conversations. Don't force them. They'll come to it in their own time.
- 'If there are people you miss, you can talk about them any time' – never make it taboo to talk about Mum or Dad or anyone else important they are missing. Talk about them often. Children are often afraid of losing their memories of their parents or siblings. If you can, remind them of how much they had in common, whether it be fashion sense, musical ability or a cheeky smile.
- 'You're not better than those who died' – remind your children that their survival doesn't mean that they have a particular burden to fulfil. It's OK just to be them, whoever they are. What happened was random. People survived or died by pure luck. This is frightening, but probably easier to bear than the idea that the dead somehow deserved what happened.
- 'We have two choices: to give into despair or to work together to make a better world' – we're all working together now. The human race isn't over. There are good things coming. And never ever stint on reminding kids how much you love them.

ROFFLENET: YOUR FRIEND IF YOU'RE ALONE

Some of you may have read this chapter with sadness. Perhaps there simply are no living people near you. You have been able to survive and escape your siege, you have set up a secure dwelling and daily walks . . . but everyone is dead. The journey to any nearby community may be fraught with dangers. The Ministry is aware of people in this predicament – on rocky islands off the coast of Britain, for example, or in mountainous regions ringed by zombie-ridden towns.

If this is your situation, you have our sympathy. We are trying hard to reach you, but we are aware that it may be some years before we're able to make contact with every person in the country. If you have found this book from one of our airdrops, we are sorry that we cannot land and rescue you. We will come for you in time.

Until then, please make use of ROFFLENET if you can. It is a global standard replacement for the Internet of old. It's not fast – it's more like a 'bulletin board' from the 1970s and may take several minutes to load a single page of text. But it will make you feel less alone. You will be able to swap recipes, tips and techniques with other survivors. You will be able to tell your story to people who want to hear it. You will be able to take part in a 'community' of other isolated individuals, and even participate in 'virtual' events such as celebrations, storytelling evenings and races. ROFFLENET is accessible from any home computer, using the instructions provided on page 202 to set up a basic receiver/transmitter. We want to hear from you.

▲ ROFFLENET SYMBOL SPRAYED ON WALL

CASE STUDY: Janine De Luca

I was quite a loner before the apocalypse. I suppose I liked it that way. I had worked for the government in the time before – a rather boring bureaucratic position, there's not much to say about it. I was living alone in an isolated farmhouse after some career setbacks, and had got quite set in my ways. I like routine, order, discipline and predictability.

Of course, the zombie apocalypse has put paid to all that! At first, a few survivors arrived at my farmhouse, hoping to stay for a few nights. But, well set up as I was, I soon found myself hosting a large number of survivors in makeshift huts and tents on my farm. And I've become the de facto leader of our community.

Some tensions have been mitigated from the start by my ability to run a disciplined organization. I began by organizing rosters for various communal tasks – I think that it gave the people around me a sense of hope and purpose to be told what to do and set to work. One element that's been particularly interesting to me is finding useful work for members of the community who might have seemed a bit hapless. I have to confess that 'people skills' aren't my strong suit! But there are people in our community who are good at encouraging, supporting and mentoring others, and I've been delighted to see them bloom in their new roles.

One facet of our new life which has been hard for me is the constant enforced social time. I've often found myself sitting at a communal table almost deafened by the constant din, exhausted by the demands of those around me and unable to find a moment to think.

It's been very important for me to keep my bedroom very much out of bounds for any but invited guests. If I retreat there with the door closed, I will not be disturbed and will have time for reading and strategic thinking. I would also say that as time's gone on my social skills have improved – not a change I would have expected before the zombie apocalypse!

NOTES

SECTION 04

FIT FOR BATTLE

All information and advice contained in this chapter is intended for use in the event of a zombie apocalypse. Until that time, it is for entertainment purposes only. All weapons can be dangerous and deadly, and those described here are only for use in zombie self-defence situations. Neither the publisher nor the author makes any guarantee that any techniques described will be safe or effective in a zombie apocalypse and will not be held responsible for any loss, damage or injury which occurs.

INTRODUCTORY REMARKS

In the first place, before choosing weapons or starting to train, you must be certain to abide by the most important rule of all: obey the laws and regulations governing weapons and fighting in the place where you are. Different settlements and government-administered zones have different rules. It is your responsibility to learn what the law is where you live and to adhere to it in every detail. These laws and regulations have been imposed for a reason, and we are not in a position to understand the nuance of any situation you may find yourself in. ***Obey the laws where you are.*** It is the support of the human community you live in that will keep you safe.

It is also true that most of us are naturally peaceful people. In the time before the zombies, we would never have armed ourselves or trained to fight. And if you are lucky enough to live on one of the few islands with no zombie incursion, or if you are protected by a militia or guard, you may safely ignore this section of the book.

Few of us are that lucky today. Even so, we advise the lone survivor or even the small settlement to avoid fighting the zombies if at all possible. Clearing your area may be essential – in that case use the approved decoy-and-burn distant kill techniques suggested in Ministry Briefing no. 17: How to Dispatch a Large Horde of Zombies Safely. In all other situations our recommendation is to avoid engaging in combat with zombies; the risk of infection is too great to advise hand-to-hand combat in all but the most perilous situations.

Sadly, as we are all aware by now, it is not always possible to avoid the most perilous situations. The fighting techniques outlined in this section are a last resort, but we live in the darkest of times. You may need to go from room to room to clear an otherwise safe and defensible dwelling place of its unfortunate previous occupants. You may – despite your best efforts – have to fight off a zombie incursion into your home. You may have to dispatch a loved one whom you hoped would recover from the festering bite wound they took from the postman.

Or you may find yourself cornered by a horde while out foraging for supplies or travelling from settlement to settlement. You may be chased by a pack of fast zombies, or you may have taken shelter in a tree overnight only to find it surrounded by zombies in the morning and have to fight your way out. Most of us have experienced some version of at least one of these situations by now. If you're alive to read this book, it's because you acted on instinct, grabbed whatever was to hand and smashed until you saw the decaying brain of your undead opponent oozing out of its pulverized skull. You've been resourceful and strong – but you've also been lucky.

FIT FOR BATTLE

Our intention in this section is to help you ensure that the next time you face one of the shambling dead in unavoidable combat, you have more than luck and a particularly heavy vase on your side. We advise all survivors to familiarize themselves with the basic techniques outlined on pages 112–121.

There are more advanced skills for those who feel confident using them, but remember: the most effective fighting practice is the one that is second nature to you in an attack. Pick a method of combat that you feel comfortable with and practise it consistently. Plenty of zombies have been killed with a good lunge from a sharpened tin can nailed to a broom handle – there is no need for drop kicks or throwing daggers to keep yourself and your loved ones safe.

IT IS THE SUPPORT OF THE HUMAN COMMUNITY YOU LIVE IN THAT WILL KEEP YOU SAFE

ESSENTIALS OF ZOMBIE-FIGHTING

Fighting a zombie is not like fighting a human being. They live in our bodies but are not us. Remembering this will save your life. Forgetting it for a moment can spell death.

Consider: if in a fight with a living human you cut off both of their arms and struck them multiple times in the chest with an axe, while they only managed to inflict a tiny bite wound on your hand, you would have indubitably won the fight. In the same situation with a zombie, they would have won and you would have become another soldier in the army of the damned.

Conversely, if you are fighting a human opponent you have to consider what they are thinking and what cunning plan they may put into operation. Do they feint left intending all the while to attack from the right? Are there more of them deliberately hiding, waiting to ambush you? Are they planning to use your own strength against you if you use a full-frontal assault? None of these considerations apply to the zombie. You are more intelligent than a zombie by a considerable degree. If you're used to fighting human beings, you may find yourself overthinking the fight and getting into danger that way.

MY ZOMBIE KILL STRATEGY

....

....

....

....

....

....

....

....

....

....

....

....

....

....

The essential facts are these:

To kill a zombie, you must remove its head or destroy its brain.

If any zombie's fluids, secretions or flesh enter your bloodstream through any cut, however small, you will become a zombie. This applies equally to cuts and scrapes, to zombie-inflicted bite wounds and to zombie-splatter that enters your eyes or a small nick inside your mouth.

Most zombies move more slowly than the living, and (depending on freshness) their bodies tend to be more decayed and thus easier to destroy; you can defeat them in single combat with relative ease.

Avoid at all costs becoming hemmed in by a zombie horde with nowhere to retreat or hide. Our research indicates that more than 95 per cent of single-human-versus-single-zombie combat situations are now won by the living while only 40 per cent of encounters between a single human and a horde of more than 15 zombies end well for the human being.

For these reasons, we recommend the following strategies:

Familiarize yourself with the use of a long-handled or ranged weapon capable of destroying a zombie brain without close combat.

When fighting, wear thick clothes if at all possible, with goggles and masks if available and appropriate. This may be radically different to what you're used to if you've trained in close-combat fighting in the past. You will have to retrain your instincts.

Your best strategy if faced with a horde is to outrun it or to hide. We will also cover some features of zombie horde behaviour on page 131, and suggest ways to make effective use of the fact that zombie hordes will chase living humans.

BASIC WEAPONS TO CONSTRUCT AT HOME

The principle of zombie-killing weapon construction is simple: you need a blade sharp enough to decapitate or a weight large enough to crush, with a delivery system which ensures that the combatant need not get too close to the zombie. Of course it goes without saying that none of these weapons should be used to attack another living human – always be certain that the figure you're attacking is actually one of the living dead. The ranks of humans are thin enough without our reducing them yet further ourselves.

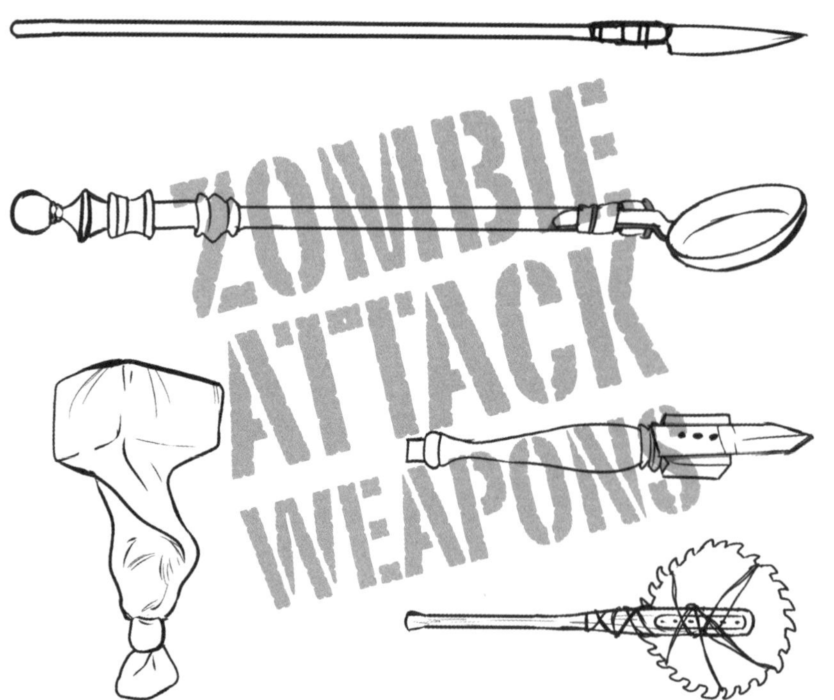

◀ **Kitchen knife lashed to a broom handle**

◀ **Heavy frying pan – or home dumb-bell – lashed to, for example, a sturdy piece of metal bedstead**

◀ **Flattened and sharpened tin can nailed to a chair leg**

◀ **Saw blade strapped to baseball bat**

▲ **Hammer or crowbar**

Sandbag (reinforced with duct tape), which can be thrown from an upstairs window (with a rope and pulley to haul it back)

Molotov cocktail (only to be used if the zombies aren't in or near to your shelter!)

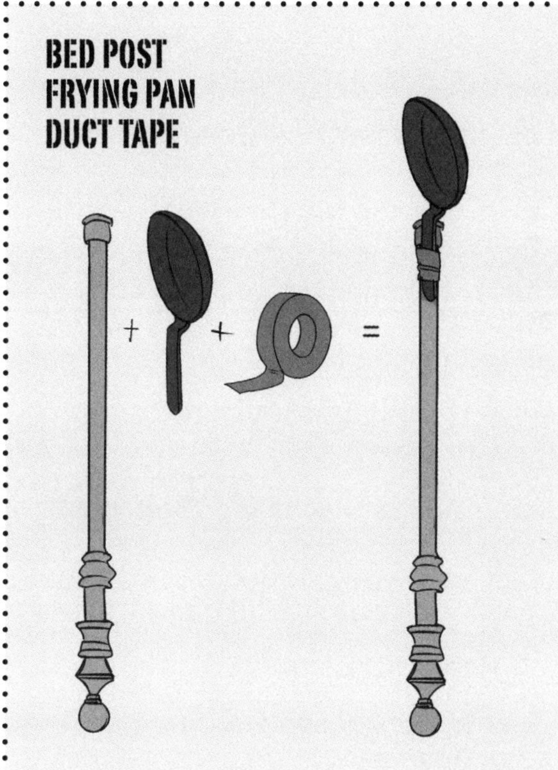
BED POST
FRYING PAN
DUCT TAPE
+
+
=

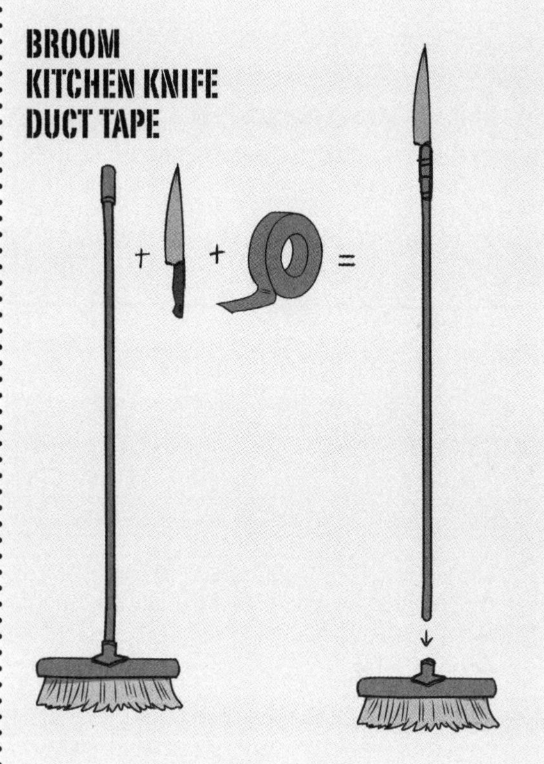
BROOM
KITCHEN KNIFE
DUCT TAPE
+
+
=

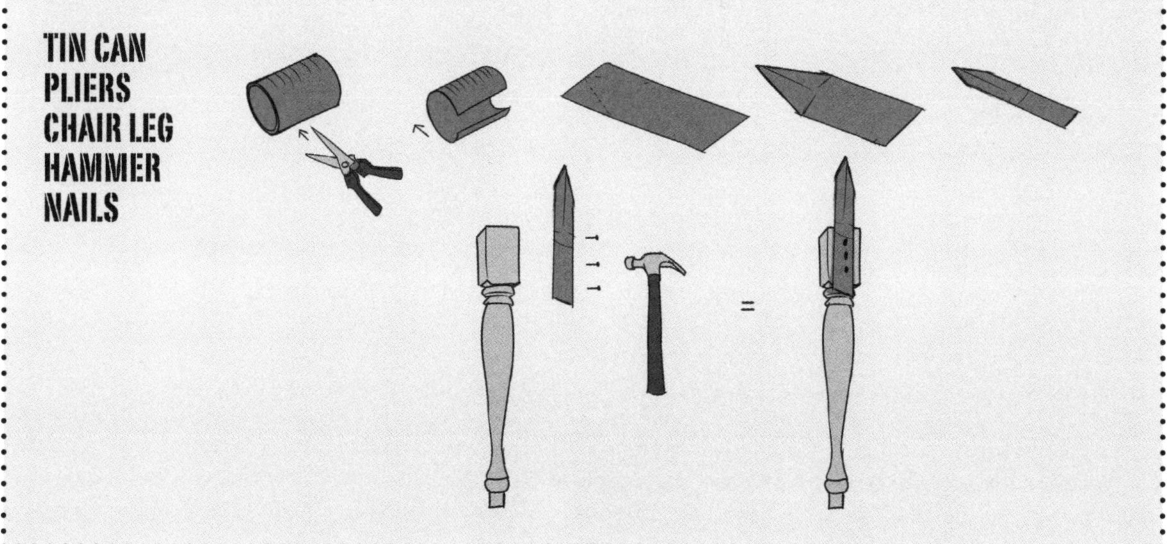
TIN CAN
PLIERS
CHAIR LEG
HAMMER
NAILS
=

TRAINING EXERCISES TO IMPROVE YOUR COMBAT SKILLS WITH A BASIC WEAPON

Practise your skills with a blunt stick at least every other day.

To begin our recommended regime, build a dummy from old rags, thick sacking, pillows or blankets, fastened with tape or rope. Try to make sure that the dummy has a discernible head, torso and lower limbs. You may like to draw a zombie face on it, for extra verisimilitude. Hold your weapon with both hands – your blows are likely to be more forceful. Consider the ways you can move your weapon to generate force: rotation, swipes up and down, jabbing it forward and so on.

Set a timer for 30 seconds and practise each of the following movements in turn, taking time to recover whenever you need to, and at least a few minutes of rest between each full set. If you have only a short amount of time to practise, focus on attacking the head and neck with each of these movements. If you want to perform a particularly intense training session, make each type of strike on each of the dummy's body parts.

Diagonally sweep from a low position to a high one – from foot to hip on the dummy. Alternate between starting from the left and from the right, aiming to make hard contact with the weapon against the dummy. Be sure to shift your weight down so as not to destabilize yourself with the force of hitting.

Diagonally sweep from a middle position – from hip to shoulder and from hip to foot on the dummy. Alternate between starting from the left and from the right, aiming to make hard contact with the weapon against the dummy. Think about generating rotational force, as if you had a stick directly through your centre. You should be able to generate a large amount of power with this movement!

Diagonally sweep from a high position downwards – from above the shoulder to hip on the dummy. Alternate between starting from the left and from the right, aiming to make hard contact with the weapon against the dummy. This can be useful to break bones such as the collar bone or to attack lower limbs.

Jabs are useful to repel zombies and cause rapid damage. If the zombie is well-rotted, jabs may even cause it to disintegrate. Spend the full 30 seconds on each body part, jabbing from a straight position and thinking about what damage you can do to eyes, nose, jaw, etc. You will need to adjust your body position as you strike lower down on your enemy, so think about widening your stance and dropping your weight.

Swipe down from overhead. This is a particularly useful movement for attacking the head. Bring your weapon as high as you can, and sink your weight into it as you bring it down, generating as much force as you can.

ADVANCED EXERCISES TO IMPROVE YOUR COMBAT PERFORMANCE

Your performance in combat with zombie assailants will be greatly enhanced if you have more power and control in your upper body. Continue with your regular routine of running, squats and so on to maintain strength in your lower body, but if you want to take your upper-body strength to the next level, train to perform one-arm push-ups and pull-ups.

One-arm push-ups

Once you've improved your strength enough to do 15 regular push-ups, you're ready to start working on the one-arm push-up.

Start by finding yourself a table or bench about 50–70cm from the ground. Can you do a push-up on it with one arm? If not, keep working on your regular push-ups until you're able to push up from a 70cm bench with one arm. If you have access to weights, you could use them to perform resisted elbow extensions to improve your performance here.

- The technique for one-arm push-ups is to have your feet about 50cm apart for balance, and to ensure that you keep your hips level and don't let your bottom come up. Your body should be a straight line.

- Work, over the course of weeks or months, towards being able to do a set of ten push-ups with each arm at this height.

- Then find a table, workbench or other steady surface that is approximately 10–15cm lower. Repeat the process until you can once again perform a set of ten one-arm push-ups on each side.

Keep lowering the bench by 10cm or so every time you're able to do a set of ten one-arm push-ups with each arm. Eventually you will be strong enough to do them on the ground.

Pull-ups

Your first challenge is to find something horizontal that's suitably sturdy to do your pull-ups on. It must be high enough for you to hang from with locked-out arms without having to bend your legs very much. It should have a good surface, from which your hands won't slip. And it clearly needs to be capable of bearing your weight! We would suggest that a solidly constructed door frame or set of banisters can be a good option, but please make sure you're safe before attempting this exercise; we don't know how your home or zombie-shelter is constructed!

- Begin by increasing your strength with the table-top pull-ups described on page 28. Before you start training for a pull-up, you should be able to do a set of ten table-top pull-ups with your body straight, your feet and legs fully extended from your body. Only then are you ready to move on to pull-ups.

- Find a sturdy object (such as a chair or step-stool) high enough that you can step on it and reach your 'pull-up bar', with your arms bent and your chin just above it. Your palms should be facing away from you.

- Step off the chair, and using your upper-body strength, try to lower yourself down as slowly as you can. That is, you are beginning to train by doing the reverse of the motion you're eventually aiming for – lowering yourself down rather than pulling yourself up. At the start this will be difficult, but try to do it ten times, going as slowly as you can, and making sure to retain control.

- It might take a month or more, but eventually you should be able to lower yourself for a count of ten, step on to the chair to rest for another count of ten, and repeat that ten times.

- At this point you are ready for full pull-ups. To begin training to do full pull-ups, hang from the bar with your arms straight, a bit more than shoulder-width apart, but keep tension in your shoulders so that you are pulling your head up between your arms slightly, rather than simply dangling in this position floppily.

- Start the pull from your shoulder blades – think about pulling them down and together – and then pull with your arms to raise yourself so your chin is just above the bar. Lower yourself down with control.

- The sets and reps you do and the rest times you take will be up to you – it is better to perform one pull-up in full control than several in an explosive way that could potentially lead to injury.

You might start with five single pull-ups with two-minute rests in between each one, then eventually move to five sets of five with only a minute's rest between. Eventually you'll be able to perform sets of ten, and your zombie-killing power will have increased a great deal.

FIGHTING STYLES FOR A SINGLE COMBATANT

You may already be skilled in a martial art, in kickboxing, boxing or another combat style. We would urge you to try to forget much of what you have learned, when fighting zombies. Of course, your physical fitness will still be an asset. But as explained on page 112, fighting the undead is very different to fighting the living.

- While zombies sometimes appear to feel pain, insofar as they may moan or grunt when they are dealt a blow, damage that would be very painful for a living human does not slow a zombie. You may have been taught in a self-defence class to aim for painful areas: the solar plexus, a side kick to the knees, the genitals. These strategies will not serve you when fighting a zombie.
- Zombies, as far as Ministry research has been able to ascertain, are guided as much by sense of smell as by sight. Putting out their eyes will not stop them coming for you.
- Your most significant weapon is your intelligence. In this alone you are far superior to a zombie. They are mindless creatures that respond predictably to a small range of stimuli: motion, noise, the scent of flesh. You can use this to your advantage.

HERE IS OUR FIVE-POINT PLAN FOR REMAINING ALIVE IN COMBAT WITH A ZOMBIE

ADJUST...

your situation. Is there any way for you to change the field of combat? You don't want to be fighting in close quarters if you can avoid it. The zombie will chase you if you move, and this can be used to your advantage.

LINE 'EM UP

Your best bet is, if possible, to arrange to fight the zombies one by one, rather than in a great mass. Try to find a corridor or other space down which they will have to come single-file towards you.

INSPECT...

the condition of the zombies in front of you. Are they well rotted? If so, you may be safe to attack with a simple jabbing motion, aimed at removing the head from the body. Are they fresh? Then you will need to use a blade or a crushing weapon.

VIOLENCE...

will be necessary, but you should husband your physical resources carefully, especially if you'll be dispatching a large group of zombies. Use the most economical movements you can: side swipes to the head and sharp downward cleaver blows.

ESCAPE...

as soon as you can. Don't be a hero. Don't try to deal with a large horde by yourself. As soon as you are safely able to do so, get away from the horde and run.

TWO-PERSON TRAINING

Training with a partner can be particularly useful. Have your friend dress up in pillows and blankets and mimic the motions of a zombie. Then use a light stick – rather than the heavy weapon you use for training on a dummy – to practise attacks on them.

It can be particularly useful to practise in an abandoned house, mimicking the process of clearing out a dwelling in search of supplies. Have your friend hide somewhere in the house without telling you where, and then proceed to 'clear the house' room by room, without knowing when they are likely to suddenly leap out at you.

You may like to frame this training as a game, in the following way:

Cover your friend's head in a white paper hat. Construct the hat from paper and tape – make sure it covers their face (with mouth and eye holes!), back of the head and neck. Instead of your usual weapon – cleaver on a broomstick or similar – take a small, light stick and tape a marker pen to the end of it. Apply lipstick to your friend's lips – this should be a bright colour.

You should then commence your search of the house, not knowing where your friend will be hiding.

When the 'zombie' jumps out at you – which may be when you enter the room 'it' is in, or when 'it' hears you searching and creeps up to attack – the battle commences.

Ministry research suggests that it takes an average of ten blows to the head and neck to render a zombie dead. You, the 'human', must attempt to make ten marks with your pen on the zombie's white paper hat.

Meanwhile, the 'zombie' is attempting to plant its bright lipstick kiss on the 'human' – either on flesh or on a piece of clothing so thin that it would provide no protection against a zombie bite.

If the 'zombie' succeeds in planting one kiss, 'it' has won. If the 'human' makes ten distinct marks on the 'zombie's' paper hat and mask, the 'human' has won.

This game has the benefit of training both parties. The 'human' gets experience of simulated combat, while the 'zombie' gains valuable insights into combat from the perspective of the living dead. Please make sure that you use safe marker pens and that you do not injure each other while playing this game – we cannot afford any unnecessary casualties among the ranks of the living!

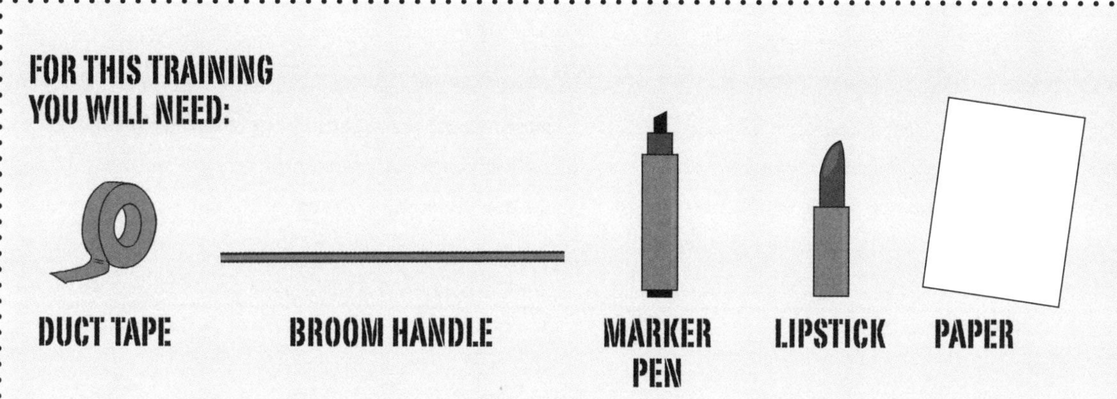
FOR THIS TRAINING
YOU WILL NEED:
DUCT TAPE
BROOM HANDLE
MARKER
PEN
LIPSTICK
PAPER

TWO-PERSON FIGHTING STYLES

If one human is smarter than the average zombie horde, imagine how much more intelligent two capable human beings are! This should be your watchword when you go into combat as a team against several zombies. While a single combatant is likely to be overwhelmed by a horde of six or more, our analyses have shown that a team of two people has the advantage – if both parties know what they're doing! – over a horde of up to 40 zombies.

CHASE-AND-AMBUSH STRATEGY

Many teams have developed this simple two-person fighting style without any instruction. It relies on the fact that zombies will follow any human, and that they are somewhat slower than humans. They are also completely oblivious to the fates of their fellow zombies – even seeing another zombie get killed in front of them will not make them slow down or change direction.

So, in the chase-and-ambush strategy, one member of the team conceals themselves in a useful zombie 'kill box'. This may be a high place with a good supply of rocks to drop on the zombies, an excellent place to fire a rifle or crossbow from, or simply a well-defended ledge from which the zombies can be attacked with a cleaver on a stick. The other member of the team encourages the zombies to chase them towards the kill box – having ensured that there's an easy method of escape for an agile human! Perhaps a rope ladder that can quickly be withdrawn or a hand up on to a rocky ledge. This leaves the zombies in the pre-designed kill box, ready to be relieved of their miserable, rotting lives.

THE MCSHELL MANOEUVRE

Named after its inventor, this second two-person fighting style is a little more complex but will yield excellent results when correctly deployed. It relies on the fact that zombies do not operate like any other predator. Most predators will chase after the slowest members of the group: the young, the old, those that are already sick or injured. They make the easiest prey. Zombies are not like this. They chase after any human that moves. They simply do not appear to have any instinct to go after weak human prey rather than strong; they will go towards whoever is nearest. And this leaves them with an intriguing weakness: when two humans run away from the zombies at precisely the same speed in different directions, the zombies will become confused and will shamble straight forward.

Examine *Figure 1* closely to familiarize yourself with this strategy. Two runners begin at point A, the starting point. There are zombies behind them. Runner 1 runs diagonally to the left. Runner 2 runs diagonally to the right. It is crucial that the two runners match their speeds evenly, and that there are no other living humans in the field of vision. Zombies will chase after whichever human is nearest, but if there are two humans receding in different directions at the same speed . . . the expected zombie trajectory is not towards Runner 1 or Runner 2 . . . but towards point B.

When correctly deployed, this strategy can be extremely effective. If point B is a cliff-edge or the open gate of a fenced area, many zombies can be killed or safely herded without either runner coming anywhere near them. The McShell manoeuvre takes practice and a pair of runners in close sympathy with each other but in skilful hands it is very valuable.

Figure 1

Figure 2

WE WOULD ENCOURAGE YOU TO PRACTISE IT AS MUCH AS YOU CAN.

SPECIAL SKILLS

There are a variety of special combat skills which have proven useful to survivors. We cannot give adequate training in each of these skills in this book, although we have produced a series of pamphlets for those who are interested in them. We mention these special skills briefly here to give you a sense of the wide and deep training you could undertake and to inspire you to join or form your own local groups to hone your abilities.

ARCHERY

Once, archery was the pride of Britain. It was the chief weapon of English armies from the 14th century until the invention of pistols. It was with the longbow that the English army fought and won the Battle of Agincourt; it was instrumental in the Hundred Years War and for many centuries regular longbow training was part of the culture of this country. By making and using your own longbow, you will be participating in a tradition ancient to the United Kingdom.

Archery is an exceedingly valuable skill against zombies, particularly using the longbow, which delivers a shattering blow from a great distance and can even pierce armour. A longbow bolt to the head will kill a zombie instantly, as it destroys much of the brain. The arrows can be retrieved, cleaned carefully and used again. Dip the tips of your arrows into a flammable material and set them on fire before you let them loose and you can destroy an entire horde without ever putting yourself at risk.

If you are able to learn to pull a bow and shoot an arrow, we would encourage you to do so. If you have even a modicum of crafting ability, we would urge you to learn to make bows and arrows. Gun ammunition will run out eventually. Petrol for motorized vehicles is in short supply. But this country is even now being reclaimed by the forest.

In 20 years, large swathes of this land will be covered by trees. The material for archery will always be with us – and with it, continued protection from zombie attack.

USING PALAEOLITHIC WEAPONS

We have much to learn from our hunter-gatherer ancestors. Their ancient technology of flint-knapped blades attached to spear handles is the basis of the modern sport of javelin-throwing. Their skills with slingshot and stones were able to fell elephant or bison at a distance of several hundred feet. You need give but a moment's thought to the matter to understand what a heavy spear or expertly targeted stone hurled from a slingshot would do to a zombie's brain.

If you wish to learn to use a slingshot yourself, we advise making one using surgical tubing, if any is available, or an exercise 'stretch band'. You may also be able to repurpose an irreparable tyre inner tube as the rubber portion of the slingshot.

These weapons take a great deal of practice to use with accuracy – and it's very important to be sure if you're throwing a heavy spear that you won't hit another human! But if you have a good open field to practise in, we highly encourage you to investigate this type of weaponry. Like arrows, rocks and flints aren't likely to run out.

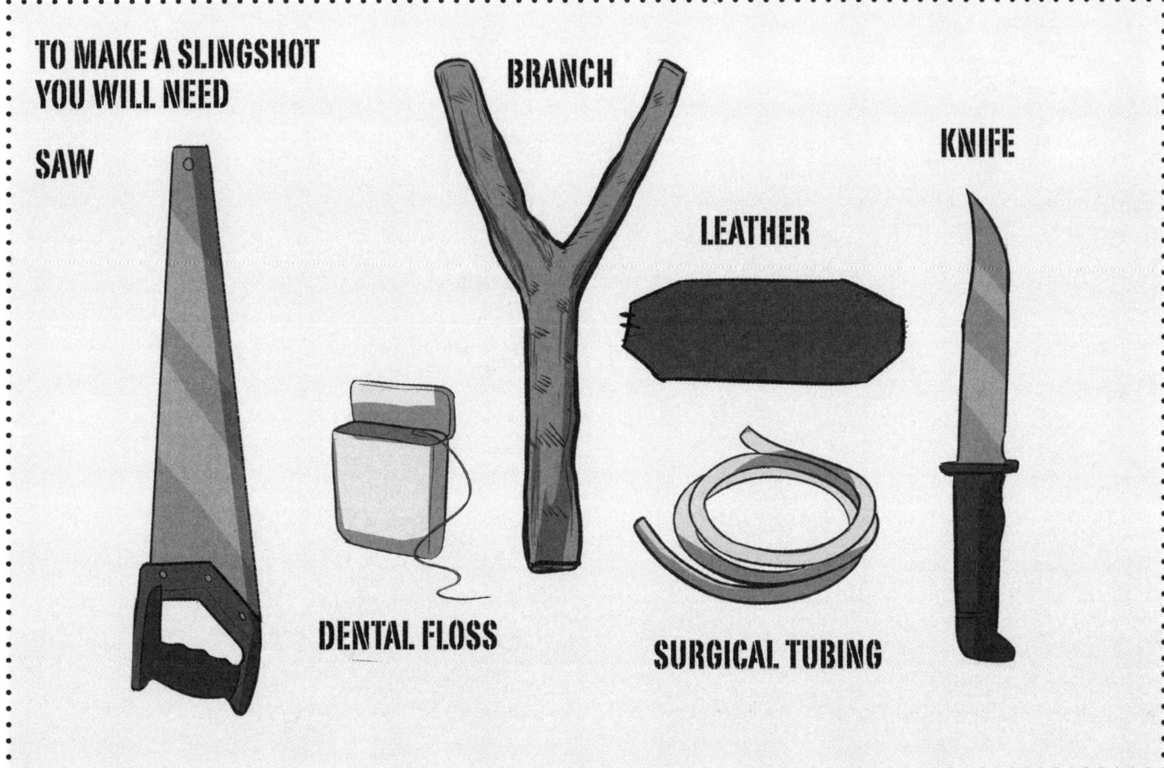

HOW TO MAKE A SLINGSHOT

1. Take a branch

2. Choose a strong 'Y' shaped piece

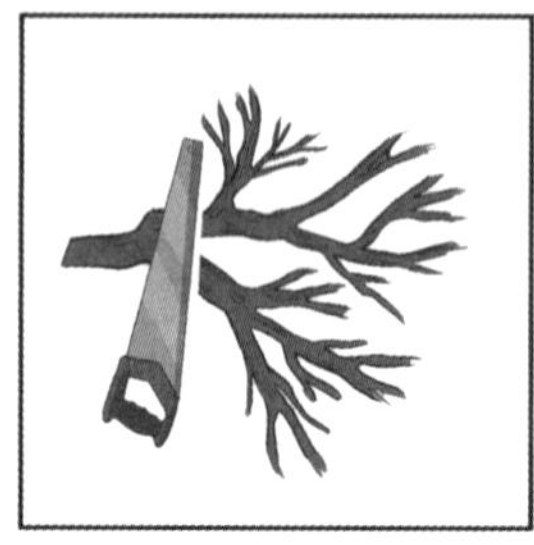

3. Saw off branch

4. Trim excess twigs to leave 'Y' shape

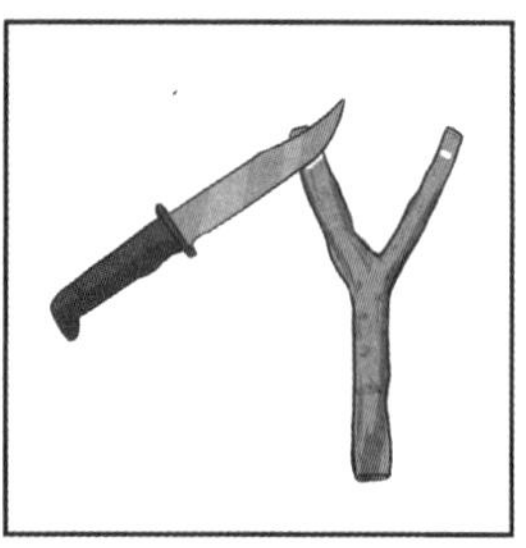

5. Cut notches for tubing

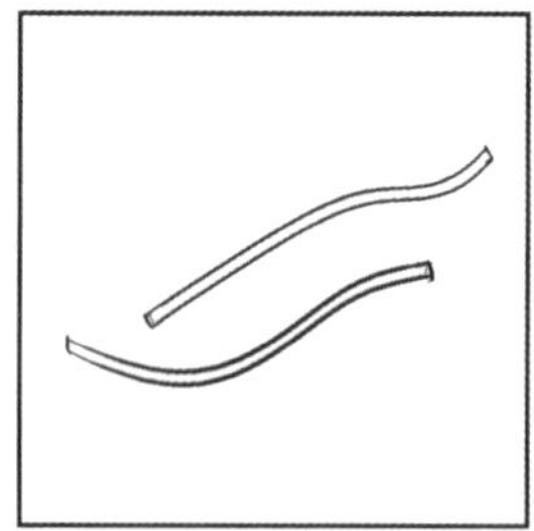

6. Cut two lengths of tubing

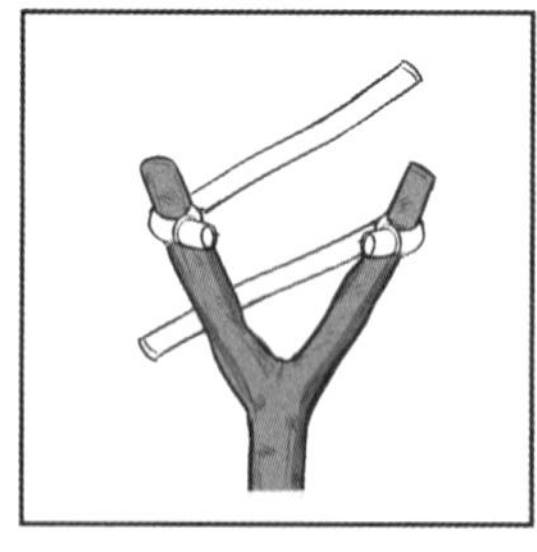

7. Attach firmly to branch

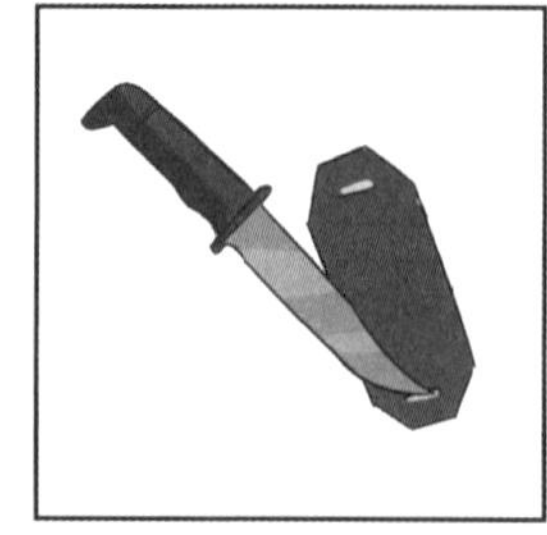

8. Cut slits in leather

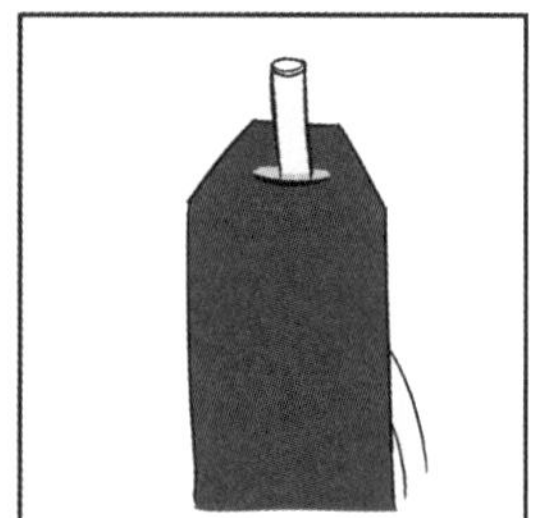

9. Pass tubing through slits

10. Attach firmly

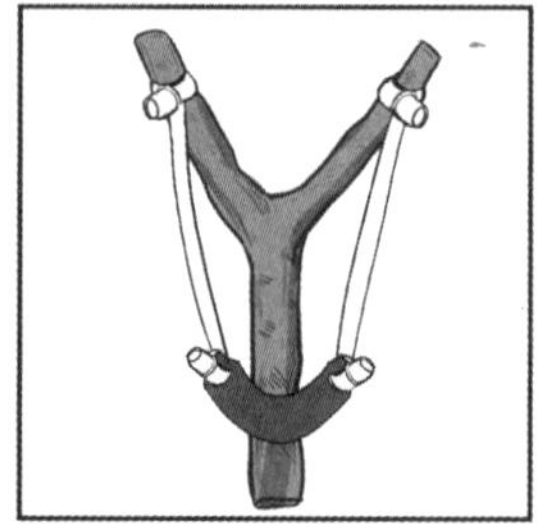

11. Your slingshot is ready to use

USING DOGS

The dog has been 'man's best friend' since long before the end of the last ice age. There is good evidence that dogs and human beings have influenced each other's evolution. And, with so many humans dead, there is no shortage of dogs in need of a good home and a loving mistress or master. Most importantly of all: a dog cannot be infected by the zombie virus. They can bite zombies with no danger of infection. This fact alone makes a dog a potentially invaluable ally in the fight against the zombie plague.

The training of dogs is a subject far beyond the scope of this book. Much has been written about it, and any foraging trip to a library or bookshop will unearth useful material. There are also ROFFLENET groups to join to learn about the care and training of a dog. Taking on a dog is, of course, a serious responsibility. A dog is for life, not just for the zombie apocalypse.

CASE STUDY

Mr ED, who describes himself as a 'wanderer', writes to tell us: 'My dog, Bonnie, has saved my life more times than I can possibly count. She's a mutt – a collie cross, and I'm pretty sure there's some German shepherd in there too. In the early days of the apocalypse, she could tell that there was a zombie nearby more quickly than I could; it's the sense of smell dogs have. We all know zombies have that weird scent – I reckon Bonnie can smell it a mile or more away. She didn't need much encouragement from me to go for their throats – sometimes she's taken the head clean off, and sometimes she's weakened the neck enough that I could get the head off with just one swing of a machete. She's held back zombies that were attacking me, she's weaved among them to trip them up, she's barked to alert me that zombies were concealed nearby, she's dug up crawlers and worried at them until their necks broke. She's a wonder. I don't think there's a person in the world I love more, or have more reason to be grateful to than Bonnie.'

FENCING & SWORD FIGHTING

You might be tempted to train in fighting with bladed weapons. If you are able to develop sufficient skill to take off a head with one slash, these weapons can indeed be formidable. The Ministry has heard, for example, of a family of sisters from Hertfordshire whose training and skill with swords and knives has kept them and their husbands safe from zombie attack. If you're able to emulate this admirable example, and have the swords to do so, by all means train to slay zombies with blades.

But most people are untrained in sword fighting. For the untrained, swords are unwieldy weapons, heavy and difficult to use very accurately. This means that it is all too easy to do two fatal things: to cut oneself, and to slash at the zombie in such a way as to create a spray of blood, viscera and tissue. This is, self-evidently, an extremely serious infection risk.

If trapped with a horde of zombies – for example a group of zombified sightseers – in a castle with an array of medieval weapons at your disposal, the Ministry recommends that you pick up a mace or other club-type weapon in preference to a sword. Even an axe – with its single-bladed edge – is less likely to give you the opportunity to cut yourself or other humans!

CASE STUDY

Mrs CL of Longbourn sends us the following account of her experience: 'My husband and I were visiting a stately home when we were attacked by a horde of zombified builders – unfortunately for us they were all rather strong! We rushed towards the Great Hall where we'd seen a variety of weapons displayed on the wall, as is common in these old houses. I grabbed a giant hammer, stood on a table with my legs well out of the zombies' reach and began smashing their brains in. It's quite good fun when you get a rhythm going! Unfortunately, my husband was always a bit over-keen on impressing me and he picked up a longsword that was a little too heavy for him and rushed towards the zombies. I tried to tell him to stand well back, but it was too late. He skewered three zombies on his sword very well, but couldn't get the damned thing out of them again. The horde fell on him and pulled him to pieces before I could bash their heads in with my hammer. He never was a very sensible man, I'm sorry to say, though I do miss him.'

FIGHTING IN EXTRAORDINARY CIRCUMSTANCES

ESCAPING FROM A HORDE

There's nothing more dangerous than a true horde. The largest zombie packs ever observed have been composed of more than 4,000 individual zombies moving as one. If you've ever faced an army of zombies of this magnitude, you'll know terror. A large zombie horde can tear through buildings, demolish security fences and destroy anything in its path.

Your safest strategy is to stay far away from a horde. But what if you can't? If a derelict building bursts open, and it turns out that thousands of people had taken shelter in it and are now zombified?

Remember that every horde is composed only of individuals, each one of which is neither as strong as nor as clever as you. Hide, if you possibly can and if you think that the building you're in will survive an onslaught. If there's nowhere to hide, get to the edge of the horde as quickly as you can. Look for a wall to cling to, a small alleyway to sneak down. Look for eddies and changes of flow in the horde which will allow you space to move. If you are trapped in the centre of a horde, you should move slowly as zombies do themselves, because there's some suggestion that this will make them less likely to home in on you as prey.
It's not impossible to cut a path out through a horde, depending on what you're armed with. If you have an automatic weapon or a chainsaw, or if you're driving an armoured vehicle, then take a sighting of a tall building or other landmark in the distance and keep pushing towards it, cutting down all the zombies in your path. That way, if you become turned around in the fight you'll still know which way to head.

If you have anything that can make a noise or create a distraction, you might be able to use it to escape. One of the most effective strategies we've heard of is a survivor of a zombified school who attached a noisemaking device to a zombie teacher; this device encouraged the other zombies to chase the zombie teacher while the human survivor made her escape. You could use a grenade or other explosive to make a loud noise on one side of a building while you escape in the other direction.

In general, once you're engaged in a fight with a zombie it's best to finish the creature off if you can. But in the case of a horde, do not be tempted to turn back to 'finish the job'. Keep moving. Report the location of any horde of more than 100 zombies to the Ministry via ROFFLENET. Hordes larger than 1,000 zombies will receive special priority codes and local settlements will be notified.

ESCAPING A FIELD OF CRAWLERS

Perhaps you wandered in unwisely and have only now noticed the forest of dead hands all around you, grasping for your living flesh. Perhaps you spent the night in a tree and you're now surrounded by the heads and torsos of zombies, clacking their teeth together, eager to taste a mouthful of you. Or perhaps you want to clear out a field that would otherwise be useful agricultural land.

In all cases, sturdy boots are a major advantage. Crawlers aren't dangerous per se – they can't chase you, they can't grapple with you. They can of course trip you, and many people have died this way. So watch your footing.

If you have a sturdy pair of boots and you're trying to escape a field of crawlers, you're best advised to tread carefully, moving neither too slowly nor too quickly and, where possible, stepping directly on top of the skulls of the zombies. That way you know that you've avoided their teeth! If you're trying to clear a field, our recommendation would be to catch and incinerate the crawlers, preferably using farm or building equipment to pick them up, to avoid contact with them. The gold standard is to use a mechanical digger to pick up the crawlers and deposit them into a skip, then incinerate the contents of the skip.

If you're trying to escape a field of crawlers and you're worried about the quality of your footwear, take off any outer layers of clothing you can and tie them securely around your feet – zombie teeth are no sharper than human teeth and should not be able to penetrate several layers of cloth quickly. Then run out of the area as fast as you can – without falling over!

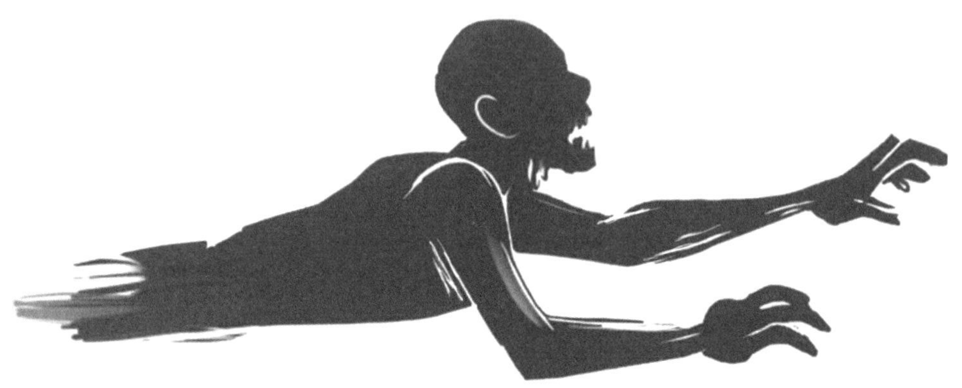

CHILD ZOMBIES

Combat against child zombies is undoubtedly distressing. Most normal people dislike it, with a substantial proportion feeling traumatized by the whole business (see next section).

Sometimes a large number of child zombies must be dispatched quickly. We strongly recommend that no one who knew the children when they were living humans be involved in this procedure. It is preferable not to involve anyone who was a parent, or anyone who feels they may be very adversely affected by the operation, although we understand this is not always possible.

If possible, the whole building containing the child zombies should be incinerated. This is our top-line recommendation.

If it is not possible to burn down the whole building, send in adults in groups of four, to keep watch for each other, moving in tight formation. In combat, child zombies are often more nimble than adult zombies – they tend to move more quickly, and can hide in awkward spots. If going into combat against child zombies, it is more imperative than ever to wear proper body armour; these zombies will not be able to deliver as violent a blow as adult zombies but their teeth can sink through flesh with just as much ease. Combine this with the very natural distaste most combatants will have for hurting a child zombie and they can prove more deadly than adults.

It is vital to fight as a group. Remind one another again of the truth we all know – you're not killing children, you're killing the virus that has already killed these children, and in doing so you're making the world safer for the children that remain.

If any of your party seems on the verge of succumbing to unbearable grief, or seems to be relating to the zombie children in any way as 'real' children, immediately call a halt to the operation and withdraw.

POST-BATTLE MENTAL HEALTH CARE

There is no question that fighting zombies is difficult emotionally as well as physically. Simply seeing zombies is terrifying and emotionally draining. For most psychologically normal people it is devastating to hack the head off a corpse which was once a living, breathing human with dreams and loves and secret fears, just like you and me.

First-line response after a zombie fight should be to allow time for rest and recuperation. Each of us should assess for ourselves what kind of recuperation works for us. For some it might be quiet walks or sleep. There is some evidence that physical activities which distract the body and the visual centres – a challenging sport or game of skill, for example – will help to reduce flashbacks to traumatic images.

If your community has a qualified mental health professional, they may set up times for frontline combatants to talk about what they've experienced. This will be particularly critical if you have lost a member of the community. The Ministry recommends that you should set up times and places to remember those you have lost, to talk about them and what they meant to you.

If you have no mental health professionals in your community – and even if you do! – you can set up systems to offer peer support. This may simply consist of people who have been trained in active listening, that is, to listen to stories of zombie combat without judgement and without offering advice. Active listeners simply reflect back what has been said to them, to indicate that they have heard it.

The Ministry has set up an anonymous system on ROFFLENET for survivors to share their stories with professionally trained active listeners. We encourage you to take advantage of this system if you need it. We have found that for many people it is simply too hard to tell the people they live with and see every day their stories of – for example – having had to kill friends, family, loved ones and even one's own children.

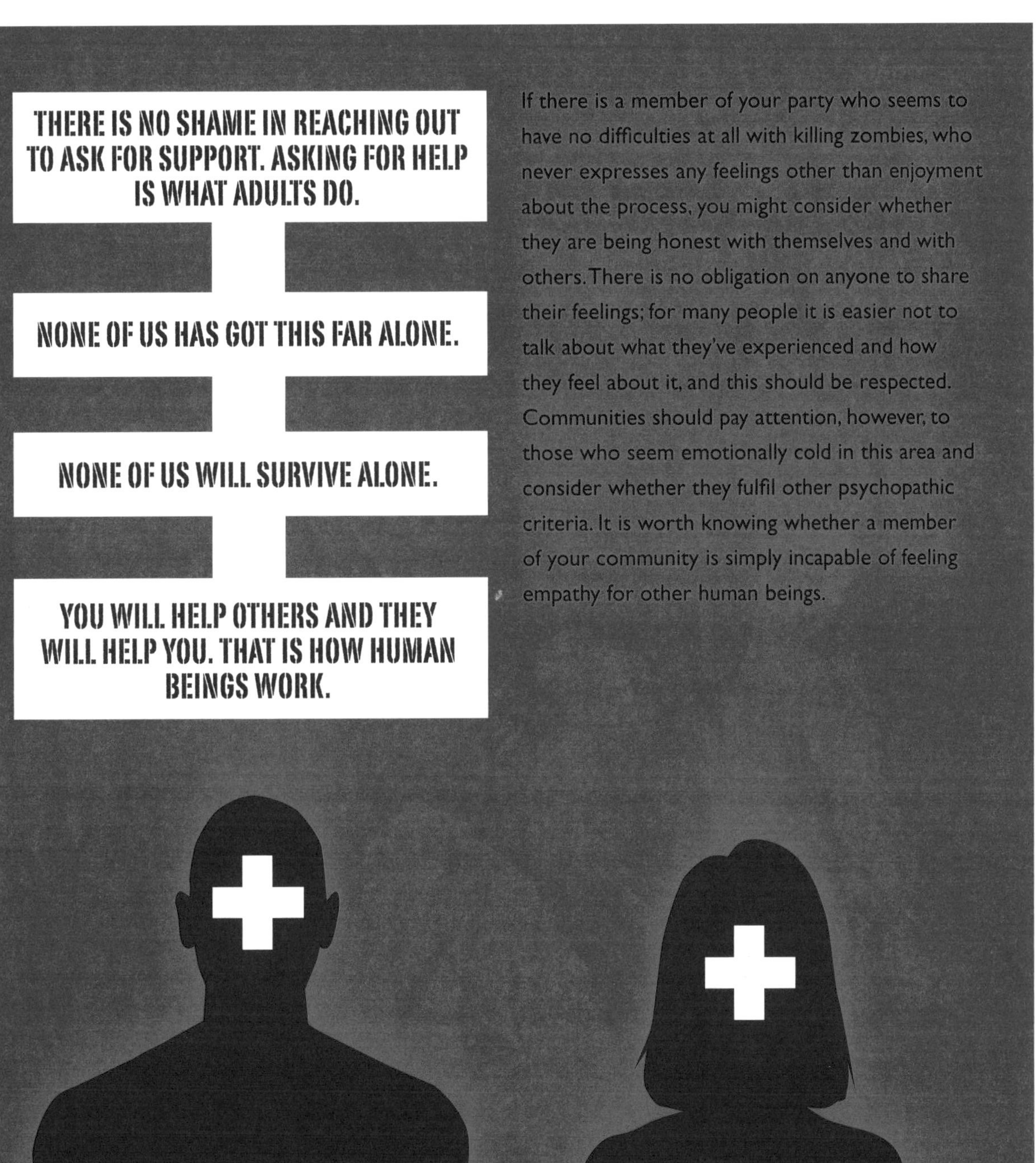

THERE IS NO SHAME IN REACHING OUT TO ASK FOR SUPPORT. ASKING FOR HELP IS WHAT ADULTS DO.
NONE OF US HAS GOT THIS FAR ALONE.
NONE OF US WILL SURVIVE ALONE.
YOU WILL HELP OTHERS AND THEY WILL HELP YOU. THAT IS HOW HUMAN BEINGS WORK.

If there is a member of your party who seems to have no difficulties at all with killing zombies, who never expresses any feelings other than enjoyment about the process, you might consider whether they are being honest with themselves and with others. There is no obligation on anyone to share their feelings; for many people it is easier not to talk about what they've experienced and how they feel about it, and this should be respected. Communities should pay attention, however, to those who seem emotionally cold in this area and consider whether they fulfil other psychopathic criteria. It is worth knowing whether a member of your community is simply incapable of feeling empathy for other human beings.

CASE STUDY: Sara Smith

Before the apocalypse I was an ordinary wife and mother. I'd worked for the military many years ago, but those times were long behind me and I was glad to be retired. I lived with my husband and my two teenage sons.

I had to kill all three of them shortly after the apocalypse began. My older son had been bitten at school. He attacked his brother and his father. I was lucky to survive. I gave them as clean a death as I could. It wasn't easy. I think for a long time afterwards – months, probably more than a year – I just felt numb. Nothing going on inside. I was grateful then for the training I'd had in my military role years ago.

FIT FOR BATTLE

They'd taught me how to survive, and that's what I did. There were things to do every day. There were rules to follow. I woke up every morning with a very obvious list of survival tasks: find water, find food, maintain my shelter, get rid of any zombies in my path. I don't know what would have happened to me if I hadn't had that training. I might just have walked into a horde.

Eventually, I fell in with another group of survivors. It was clear to me that they'd never had any training in combat and I realized that I could be the one to train them. They said afterwards that I was too tough in those early days! But they also said that I'd kept them alive. It gave me a sense of purpose. I gave them the training I wished I'd given my sons and my husband. I thought so much about what I wished they'd known, what I should have taught them.

We did daily drills in combat with wooden staves – I showed them how to take the head off a zombie without getting within reach of its arms. We trained with press-ups, squats, pull-ups and running. I remember every morning I'd say to my little group: today, you get to decide whether you live or die. Whether you want to be part of the future of the human race or just another one of those walking corpses. I don't know if that was the healthiest way to motivate anyone. But it did work.

I ask myself the same question every morning: do you want this to be the day you die? Would you be OK with that? What would you give your life for?

I've come to believe in something that's not quite spiritual, but maybe not really scientific either: the will to live. I've seen the will go out of people, seen them decide that they can't bear any of this a moment longer and give up on life. I've seen living humans who seem to have not much more animating them than the zombies; I think you can learn to see it in people's eyes.

Combat training is above all, for me, a proof to myself every day that that's not me. That I don't feel that way. When I train to fight, I'm telling myself that I believe my life is worth fighting for. That whatever has happened, and whatever I've had to do, I still belong with the living. I know that's not an enthusiastic upbeat way to think about life. But that's what I've got.

NOTES

FIT FOR SURVIVAL

INTRODUCTORY REMARKS

All the other sections in this book are aimed at the general survivor public. For each of us, even a small improvement in fitness levels can save our lives. Even just maintaining our fitness levels could make the difference between going under or surviving another day. Most of us do not need to perform great feats of endurance or skill – though many of us have surprised ourselves by finding that we can!

But this section is aimed at those who would like to take their physical fitness to the next level. Many settlements and communities have picked 'runners' or 'operatives', who are specifically given the task of running between towns to pass packages, of gathering supplies, of scouting out new areas, or of taking on the hard work of daily zombie defence.

If you have been chosen by your community for one of these roles, this section is for you. If you are living in isolated or dangerous conditions, this section is for you. If you simply have ambitions for your own fitness and want to see what your living human body is capable of as a statement of belief in humanity against the background of utter devastation, then this section is for you.

The usual caveats apply. In all cases, do not push yourself so hard or so fast that you injure yourself. You may leave yourself and your community vulnerable. You may take up a doctor's time and resources in treating you. Make your progress a little slower and more cautious than you really think you need to go.

Be aware of zombies at all times. When training hard, it is especially important to make sure that you don't end up exhausted, alone, far from home, in the pouring rain, as a horde of zombies bear down on you. If you suspect that you might be entering a hostile area, take a training buddy with you, leave information about where you're going, and be sure to carry a weapon if there are zombies in the area.

ALL-WEATHER TRAINING

The zombies don't stop for the weather, and neither do the needs of your community. If you are a runner for a settlement, you will have to be prepared to run in all weathers, and you should therefore train in all weathers.

In general, the UK's climate is fairly mild; we tend not to have extremes of either heat or cold. Even our famous rain never becomes tropically intense! However, when looting a sporting goods shop, you might like to look out for the following equipment, which will make your runs more pleasant:

SUMMER

A breathable wicking t-shirt, shorts, sweatband, a water bottle and of course the correct running shoes for your feet. Wear a hat for protection from hot sun.

AUTUMN / SPRING

Try to find a long-sleeved wicking t-shirt, along with shorts, sweatpants or Lycra running tights, as well as the correct running shoes. Lycra running tights help to protect the legs against scratches when running through bushes, and are well worth wearing, for both sexes. They also have the distinct advantage over sweatpants that – being tight-fitting – they don't give zombies any extra material to grab hold of.

RAINY WEATHER

This can of course occur in the UK in any season! If you are training to become a settlement runner, you will have to get used to running in the rain. Wear a waterproof hoodie to protect you from the worst of the weather, and do not wear any cotton clothing as it will absorb a great deal of water. Take care with your footing and don't expect to run as fast as in dry weather – you will still be fast enough to outrun the zombies, who will also suffer from the treacherous conditions. Take special care in rainy conditions if you're running in an unfamiliar place – if you don't know the paths, you're more likely to trip and fall.

WINTER

Wear the autumn or spring outfit, but add an extra outer layer, a beanie hat and a pair of gloves.

ZOMBIE BEHAVIOUR IN DIFFERENT WEATHER CONDITIONS

SUMMER

In summer, zombies tend to rot more quickly. Their movements are faster, and they can be more aggressive, but their bodies – as long as they are not very recently turned – are likely to have a more soggy texture and riper smell. This means that they are easier to detect and can usually be decapitated by a sharp blow with a heavy object.

AUTUMN / SPRING

In autumn and spring, zombies are at their deadliest. The cooler weather means they can take several weeks to reach the rotted consistency they'd reach in a few days in summer, so they are tougher to kill. They move easily. Be particularly aware of the danger posed by crawlers concealed under piles of autumn leaves. Although it's tempting, avoid running through these piles unless they've been well raked!

WINTER

In winter, zombies rot slowly. If temperatures are somewhere below zero, the zombies may remain in good active condition for many months. However, the colder temperatures mean that zombies move more slowly. The same warnings apply to snow banks as to piles of leaves – a freshly fallen snow bank may conceal a zombie ready to sink its teeth into your face, so be alert!

RAINY CONDITIONS

In rainy conditions, zombies will rot very quickly and may be covered in mould or fungus. Try to look on this as a friendly indication to you from Mother Nature that this zombie is ready to be returned to the earth!

LIST OF RUNNING SUPPLIES NEEDED:

1) ....

....

2) ....

....

3) ....

....

4) ....

....

5) ....

....

6) ....

....

7) ....

....

8) ....

....

9) ....

....

10) ....

....

UNUSUAL ZOMBIE TYPES

BE PREPARED. BE VIGILANT.

THE ZOMBIE VIRUS CAN MUTATE AND HAS DONE SO IN THE PAST.

IT INTERACTS UNPREDICTABLY WITH PRE-EXISTING HEALTH CONDITIONS OR MEDICATIONS IN THOSE WHO HAVE BEEN BITTEN.

WE SIMPLY DO NOT FULLY UNDERSTAND ALL THE DETAILS OF HOW THE ZOMBIE VIRUS WORKS OR HOW IT MUTATES.

If you see a zombie acting in an unusual manner, attempt to remain at a safe distance, observe and if possible sketch its behaviour. Warn your neighbours and the people you live with. Post the details of what you have seen on ROFFLENET or copy your sketches and send them with a traveller to the Ministry of Recovery in London. We are attempting to gather as accurate a representation of zombie activity across the country as we can; your help is vital.

See Appendix B for standard zombie classification.

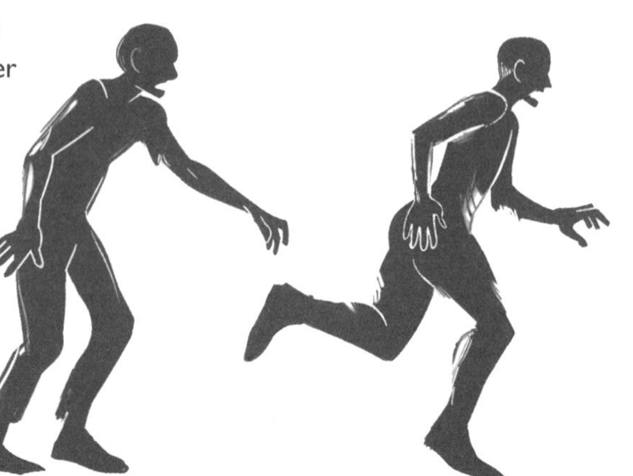

FAST ZOMBIES

Most zombies are slow. They do not derive nutrition from the food they ingest in the same manner as humans. The virus appears to hijack the digestive system in an attempt to reproduce itself; the zombie urge to bite down on living flesh seems to be more driven by the virus's drive to enter new hosts than by the desire for nutrition. Thus, most zombies experience muscle-wasting and inadequately lubricated joints, making for the typical 'shambling' gait. However, for unknown reasons some zombies certainly can and do run at high speeds. Fast zombies may not be easy to recognize if observed from a distance; they may only put on a burst of speed when in pursuit of live prey. Never assume that the peaceful slow-moving horde you see through your binoculars will remain thus if they catch sight or smell of you.

ELITE ATHLETE ZOMBIES

There is of course great variation in the physical abilities of human beings before the zombie virus invades the system. People who were unable to run in life are unlikely to be able to do so once their system has been overwhelmed by the virus! However, certain people were capable of tremendous feats in life – the Ministry has confirmed that marathon-runners, weightlifters and other elite athletes or sportspeople often retain surprising physical dexterity even when the light of life has been extinguished from their eyes forever by the horrifying plague that surrounds us. Use your observation skills: a zombie that appears to have large muscles is likely to be comparatively strong. Never let your vigilance lapse: you have no way of knowing whether the zombie standing in that supermarket aisle was a kickboxing champion in life.

S-TYPE ZOMBIES

Certain zombies have been observed to be able to carry out habitual tasks which they performed very frequently in life. The most common examples are the 'builder' zombie, which retains the ability to climb ladders, or the 'delivery person' zombie, which 'remembers' how to ring a doorbell. We suspect that 'sentient' or S-types are a variant of this; zombies which have somehow retained some muscle memory of complex tasks.

From a distance they may not even appear to be zombies – their gait and demeanour may suggest that they are a living person trapped within a horde and trying to blend in. Do not be tempted to think that they can somehow be 'saved' or 'brought back to life'; their frontal cortex has been destroyed, as in any other zombie. Reports of such zombies speaking, attempting to communicate or pleading for help are simply urban legends. The Ministry has not been able to verify any such story.

INTERVAL TRAINING: WHY DO IT?

Interval training is a particularly effective form of training, which has important applications in the zombie apocalypse. It consists, in essence, of short intervals of working at very high intensity, combined with a more moderate pace. In interval training you push yourself to the max for a short time, and then give yourself time to recover before pushing again.

Interval training is an excellent way to improve both performance and health. But it's also particularly useful now that the world has been invaded by the lumbering dead. Zombies are slower than we are, but they can threaten humans if they attack in large numbers or surprise us. When chased by a zombie horde, a minute or two of sprinting will usually take you far enough away from danger to save your life. Therefore, in our context it's particularly important to practise going 'all out' for a minute or two. If your body is used to doing this, it will have a sprint to give you at the moment when being able to run away fast will save your life.

Be aware though that intense interval training is not intended for beginners, or people who have had a long break from exercising! Although the sessions may be very short – as little as seven minutes – the intensity becomes greater as the session progresses and it's very easy to push yourself too hard and succumb to injury. Even if you have been exercising for a while and are confident in your abilities, make sure that you warm up properly before you begin.

HOW TO SET UP AN INTERVAL TRAINING PROGRAMME

Interval training was originally designed as a way of improving running performance, but you can perform interval training with any kind of exercise – any of the aerobic or strength-training exercises outlined in this book can be performed in an interval-training style. You can create your own routines using any of the exercises we've suggested.

One simple interval protocol is to perform 20 seconds of high-intensity exercise followed by 10 seconds of rest.

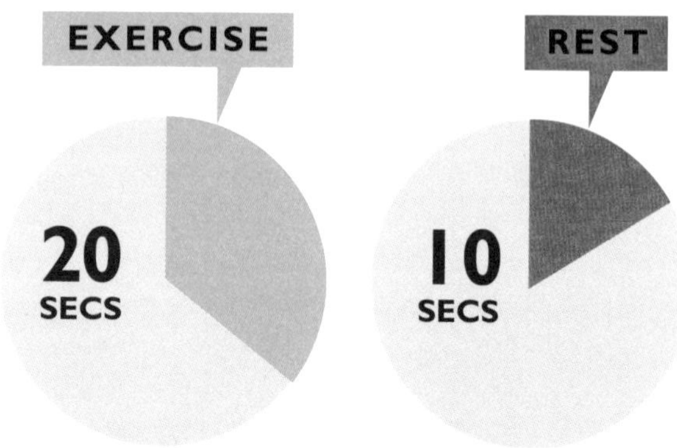

So a four-exercise session might include:

20 seconds of jumping jacks followed by 10 seconds' rest

20 seconds of squats followed by 10 seconds' rest

20 seconds of burpees followed by 10 seconds' rest

20 seconds of push-ups followed by 10 seconds' rest

You would then repeat that cycle six to eight times, for a total of 12–18 minutes of exercise. Don't be deceived! If you're working at maximum capacity for each 20-second session, this amount of exercise can feel like a very long time.

TRAINING TO RUN FOR TEN KILOMETRES

There's no one perfect level of fitness for the zombie apocalypse. And as we've said before, any improvements you are able to make to your fitness level, however small, will help to keep you alive and well through the current emergency. Your survival chances improve massively when you incorporate a small amount of exercise into an otherwise sedentary lifestyle, a greater proportional improvement than you'd get by going from 'quite fit' to 'very fit'!

Having said this, if you're relatively young and in good health, then you might set yourself a target to be able to run ten kilometres. It is a distance that will encompass a good portion of the area surrounding your community, township or living quarters, and means that you should be able to fully 'quarter the area' in each direction at least once a week (see page 59). Most townships in the United Kingdom have another township or major settlement within around ten kilometres, so being able to run this distance will mean you can take part in trade with other communities or warn another settlement of approaching danger. It is a serviceable distance to run, and is within the capacity of many.

The training programme outlined overleaf will take you from being able to run five kilometres to being able to complete the ten-kilometre distance. If you are not yet able to run five kilometres, consult the 'Beginning to run' section on page 64.

PLAN FOR 10K TRAINING			
Week	**Monday**	**Tuesday**	**Wednesday**
1		**30 min** Run for 15 min, walk for 2 min, then run for another 15 min	
2		**40 min** Run for 20 min, walk for 2 min, then run for another 20 min	
3		**30 min** Continuous run	
4		**30 min** Continuous run	
5		**30 min** Continuous run	
6		**45 min** Continuous run	
7		**30 min** Easy continuous run	

PLAN FOR 10K TRAINING			
Thursday	**Friday**	**Saturday**	**Sunday**
30 min Run for 15 min, walk for 2 min, then run for another 15 min			**3K** Continuous run
40 min Run for 20 min, walk for 2 min, then run for another 20 min			**5K** Continuous run
30 min Continuous run			**5K** Continuous run
30 min Continuous run			**40 min** Continuous run
40 min Continuous run			**50 min** Continuous run
45 min Continuous run			**10K** Continuous run
25 min Easy continuous run			**10K** Your race day!

PLAN FOR 20K TRAINING			
Week	**Monday**	**Tuesday**	**Wednesday**
1		**5K** Fast pace	**5K** Easy run
2		**5K** Fast pace	**5K** Easy run
3		**5K** Fast pace	**6K** Easy run
4		**5K** Fast pace	**6K** Easy run
5		**5K** Fast pace	**6K** Easy run
6		**5K** Fast pace	**6K** Easy run
7		**5K** Fast pace	**6K** Easy run
8		**5K** Fast pace	**6K** Easy run
9		**5K** Fast pace	**6K** Easy run
10		**5K** Fast pace	**6K** Easy run
11		**5K** Easy run	**8K** Easy run
12		**5K** Fast pace	**8K** Easy run

PLAN FOR 20K TRAINING			
Thursday	**Friday**	**Saturday**	**Sunday**
5K Easy run		**5K** Easy run	**7K** Easy run
5K Easy run		**5K** Easy run	**8K** Easy run
5K Easy run		**5K** Easy run	**9K** Easy run
6K Fast pace		**5K** Easy run	**10K** Easy run
6K Easy run		**5K** Easy run	**12K** Easy run
6K Fast pace		**5K** Easy run	**8K** Fast race pace
8K Easy run		**5K** Easy run	**14K** Easy run
8K Fast pace		**5K** Easy run	**16K** Easy run
9K Easy run		**5K** Easy run	**10K** Fast race pace
8K Fast pace		**5K** Easy run	**12K** Easy run
8K Easy run		**5K** Easy run	**12K** Easy run
8K Easy run			**20K** Your race day!

PLAN FOR 40K TRAINING			
Week	**Monday**	**Tuesday**	**Wednesday**
1		**10K** Fast pace	**10K** Easy run
2		**10K** Fast pace	**10K** Easy run
3		**10K** Fast pace	**12K** Easy run
4		**10K** Fast pace	**12K** Easy run
5		**10K** Fast pace	**12K** Easy run
6		**10K** Fast pace	**12K** Easy run
7		**10K** Fast pace	**12K** Easy run
8		**10K** Fast pace	**12K** Easy run
9		**10K** Fast pace	**12K** Easy run
10		**10K** Fast pace	**12K** Easy run
11		**10K** Easy run	**16K** Easy run
12		**10K** Fast pace	**16K** Easy run

PLAN FOR 40K TRAINING			
Thursday	**Friday**	**Saturday**	**Sunday**
6K Easy run		**10K** Easy run	**14K** Easy run
8K Easy run		**10K** Easy run	**16K** Easy run
8K Easy run		**10K** Easy run	**18K** Easy run
8K Fast pace		**10K** Easy run	**20K** Easy run
10K Easy run		**10K** Easy run	**24K** Easy run
10K Fast pace		**10K** Easy run	**16K** Fast race pace
16K Easy run		**10K** Easy run	**28K** Easy run
16K Fast pace		**10K** Easy run	**34K** Easy run
18K Easy run		**10K** Easy run	**20K** Fast race pace
16K Fast pace		**10K** Easy run	**36K** Easy run
16K Easy run		**10K** Easy run	**24K** Easy run
16K Easy run			**40K** Your race day!

BACKPACK TRAINING: WHY DO IT?

Most communities around the United Kingdom – and indeed the world! – send out regular runners or supply-gatherers to find useful items left from the time before. Even if you can only walk and carry a small number of items, you will still be useful to your community. The more you're able to carry, however, the more useful you'll be.

When you're out on a regular training run, you should get into the habit of picking up any useful supplies you see. Among the most useful are the following:

Bottled water – A vital commodity for preserving life

Medications – Any sort will be of use to someone in your community

Batteries – Light and invaluable

Food – According to the priority list on page 166. Even if your backpack is very full, you will still have room for herbs and spices, which make post-apocalyptic food more appealing

Vitamins – A vital supplement to our often-limited diets

Female sanitary products – Always welcomed by any community; light and easy to carry

Guns and ammunition – If you find them, these should always be collected and brought back to your settlement

Matches and lighters – A very useful addition to a settlement's supplies

Candles – Likewise a perpetually useful commodity, often used as currency in trading between settlements

Durable hard-wearing clothing – Can easily be placed into a backpack and will be of great use (female runners will particularly thank you for bringing home any sports bras you come across!)

Knives and other bladed weapons – Easier to carry than heavy mallets and the like and can be turned into useful anti-zombie defences

Of course, you may be sent out with other runners to find various items which your settlement particularly needs: building materials, technical supplies, weapons and so on. But even on these specific supply runs, keep your eyes open for anything else you might find.

HOW TO BUILD UP TO CARRYING A FULL BACKPACK WHILE RUNNING

1. **Begin by finding the right backpack for you.** Ideally you will find a large, comfortable backpack whose straps can be adjusted so that it fits snugly across your shoulders and does not move or rub. It should also have a waist strap that fits well across your hips, to distribute the weight across your body. Look for a bag that has a capacity of 40–60 litres.

2. **When you think you have found the right backpack for you, take it out on your regular runs empty.** Run with it for 30–60 minutes and then check to see if there are any places where it has left your skin red or sore. If it has irritated your skin when it's empty, it will probably hurt you to run with it when it's full. Give it to someone it might suit better and find another.

3. **When you are used to running with an empty backpack that does not make you sore,** slowly begin to add weight, ideally in the form of a sack of sand or gravel. If you are running three to four times a week, start by adding a single shovelful of 500g–1kg of sand to your backpack. Take the backpack on your regular run and see whether it causes any soreness or pain – you may need to find another, or to work out how to pad it more effectively.

4. **Then, every week add an extra shovelful of around that same weight until you are able to run with the full backpack.**

5. **Do not on any account be tempted to pile a lot of weight into the backpack for your first run!** The extra weight will take a toll on your joints if your body is not used to running with it.

6. **Once you are able to run easily with 10–15kg of weight in your backpack, you will be of immeasurable use to your community as a courier or supply-gatherer.**

RECONNAISSANCE

As outlined on page 56, you'll be more likely to survive the zombie apocalypse if you know the area you live in extremely well. As a settlement runner, you may often be sent out on reconnaissance missions: perhaps to monitor the movements of a nearby zombie horde, perhaps to take careful notes of the pickings in an area that is particularly rich in supplies, or perhaps to keep watch on a suspicious group of other living humans.

You will often find that you have very limited time to assess an area or a situation, and you need to report back accurately. It's very important to develop strategies that help you to remember what you've seen and to get into the habit of taking notes as soon as you are out of danger.

CASE STUDY: Mrs BR of Lancashire

I've been a runner for my township, Hollandiatown, for six months now. We're based in a line of shipping containers on the docks, which is a very defensible position and we also have all the fish we can take out of the ocean. We're very lucky!

We're surrounded by container ships with a lot of useful equipment and supplies in them – I was part of a group that found a shipment of canned fruits and vegetables that'll keep us going for the next six years if we want it to! But a lot of the crews of those ships have obviously become zombies, so we have to move quickly when we're doing a recce run. If we find anything useful, we need to be able to tell the other runners exactly where it is, so we don't lead them into unnecessary danger.

I've got into the habit of naming the rows of containers in the ships with the names of the people who lived on the street I used to live on, back in the time before. Number one is Mr Albert, number two is the Panjabi family, and so on. Then when I find something useful I imagine the person who lived in that house holding the item. So when I get back, if I've imagined Mrs Mackintosh from number 38 wrestling with an enormous tuna fish, I know that there's a crate of canned tuna in row 38!

It's apparently an old memory trick, to make a list that refers back to a place or people you know well.

RECONNAISSANCE TRAINING GAME

Even if you live in a 'safe zone' that has been cleared of zombies, it's still important to keep up your skill in reconnaissance at high speed. It will be many years – if ever! – before the on-the-ground skill of being able to rapidly assess an area and report its features accurately are no longer needed. The following training game has been used by Ministry runners to improve their skills.

1. Pick a safe route of around a mile – ideally it should be a route you do not know well. You might like to swap favourite running routes with a friend, so that you can both run a new route but one which has already been investigated and verified as safe.

2. Run the route, noting every red car you pass, whether parked, abandoned in the middle of the road, overturned and ravaged by zombies or in any other condition.

3. When you finish your route, draw a quick map of the area and mark each red car on it. If possible, note the condition of each one.

   You will probably find this very challenging on your first attempt! As time goes on, you will develop strategies for remembering the location of each one, whether that is by remembering names of roads, important landmarks, giving each car a name or a number, associating them with the name of a friend or any other memory strategy.

4. Then run your original route with your friend's map. Would you be able to find the red cars quickly and easily with the information they gave you? Was there anything essential they left out? Give them feedback on the usefulness of their intelligence, and ask for feedback on your map.

You can practise this same game many times with different features. Look for different colours of vehicle, houses with particular colour doors or with unsmashed ground-floor windows, look for postboxes, communal dustbins, recycling areas, colours of curtains in upstairs windows – you will be able to think of many different features to look for over time.

CASE STUDY Simon Lauchlan

I used to run a chain of gyms around here – I mean, near where I currently live in Abel Township. I really loved that feeling of getting stronger and faster with every workout, used to love to push myself to the max, you know? I suppose I was a gym bunny, but I also made it my life and livelihood. It makes me laugh now when I think about how I imagined I'd be safe in those gyms, that the money I'd made really meant anything. Then half the people in my gyms turned grey in one afternoon and the rest of us barely escaped with our lives. Talk about having everything taken away in an instant, right?

When I moved into Abel Township, I have to confess I felt a bit defeated, like the zombies had taken something from me personally. But I decided that I'd give Abel the best gym that any post-apocalyptic township could ever have.

We started out making equipment any way we could. Flat tyres from trucks? We can use those. Bottles from water-dispensers? We can fill them with sand and use them too. Old pieces of heavy chain that no one else is using, buckets slung from a post carried across the shoulders, punching bags made of old sacks ... I even made my own rowing machine out of some planks, with a seat and runners repurposed from some kitchen stools.

I started to run classes for people in the township who wanted to improve their fitness. If, like me, you went to every class you could before the apocalypse, you might be amazed at how much you've taken in without even realizing it; you probably have exercise advice to share. Just teach other people the things you remember being useful to you, make sure your class takes it slowly and that they stop if they're feeling any pain.
To be fair, I also really liked having an excuse to requisition some batteries to put on a few old ABBA tapes.

And I encouraged anyone who wanted a workout to volunteer for all the hard labour of building a settlement from scratch. I'd thought I was fit before, but when I saw what happened to my abs, my pecs and my glutes after days of carrying bricks, wooden beams and building materials ... well, I wondered why I'd never thought to volunteer on a building site sooner!

Not that it's all about vanity, obviously not. I'm really proud to be useful in the apocalypse, and to know that I count for something. Looking back now, I don't know if I ever really thought I counted for much before. I spent my time lifting and flexing in front of the mirror and felt like I'd accomplished something. But I'm starting to learn what real accomplishment is now. Plus I've got a couple of battle scars in various places I won't mention that I can't help feeling add to my overall appeal!

NOTES

FOOD FOR HEROES

INTRODUCTORY REMARKS

In a traditional health and fitness book from the time before, this section of our guide to healthy living would contain advice on what to eat, when, how often, what foods to combine, what to avoid, how to count calories and so on.

We do not feel this advice is appropriate in times of zombie apocalypse. We don't know what food resources you have available and we don't know your body. Some people thrive on nuts or fruits, others find these foods give them indigestion. Some like a high-protein diet, some are happiest with grains and starchy foods forming the bulk of their nutrition. Some have an ample walled kitchen garden protected from zombies, some are able to hunt deer through deserted urban wastelands, while some have been holed up for months in an abandoned liquorice and raisin factory with concomitantly limited food options. Dietary decisions are for you to make, based on your knowledge of your own body, your energy needs and the resources afforded to you by the hellscape of undying death which surrounds us all day by day.

There are a few guiding principles which we will outline across this section. Most nutritional advice concurs that eating a wide variety of foods is preferable to a narrow diet; we evolved as hunter-gatherers and with the ability to eat many different kinds of food. It may be tempting to stay indoors with a large sack of macaroni as your only sustenance but – if it is at all safe to do so – it will be better for your health to seek out a variety of foods.

In general it is wise to include as many fresh vegetables (and to a lesser extent fruits) as you possibly can in your diet – if fresh are not available, then canned or dried may be substituted. It is also wise to limit your intake of processed foods and of sugar. We understand that in a survival situation processed foods and sugary snacks may be your only source of nourishment, but we would encourage you to keep these foods for emergency zombie-survival situations only.

A long-term sustainable diet in the zombie apocalypse will be a healthy diet, being high in vegetables, fruits, wild game meat, nuts, seeds and whole grains, and very low in processed foods and sugars.

Trust yourself and your instincts. Learn to listen to your body. Eat when you are hungry. Stop when you are full, and find a way to preserve the extra portions of food for later. If a particular food seems to give you indigestion or make you anxious, or if it triggers a reaction of 'I just can't stop eating this', it is probably not good for you. You are the best judge of your own nutrition needs and you are well able to provide for yourself.

CLEAN WATER

The first necessity of life is clean drinking water. Thankfully, the time before supplied us with large quantities of bottled water, and in the early days of the infection the Ministry made water a top priority and was able to set up large tankers of drinking water with standpipes at street corners in most cities, towns and villages. As these tankers were intended for use by the whole population for several weeks, they have served the much reduced population for a longer time.

However, it is time now to think about a sustainable long-term supply of drinking water. Rainwater collection – our green and pleasant land is so largely because of our almost constant rain! – is the best resource in the first instance. Wherever you are living, in a treehouse, a suburban semi-detached house or a larger community, set up a system of rainwater collection as soon as you're able. This need not be elaborate: a tarpaulin with a hole in the middle leading to a duct-taped drainage hose piping the water to a sealed barrel is sufficient. Make sure that your water container has a lid – insects, birds or zombie parts falling in could render the water unsafe.

Boil all drinking water. Urgent Ministry testing has confirmed that a sharp boil for ten minutes ensures that even water that has contained zombie parts cannot infect the living. Solar water disinfection also kills the zombie pathogen in the water – for more details on this, we refer you to ROFFLENET advice on solar water disinfection, or to Ministry Briefing no. 54: Do Drink the Water and Breathe the Air. These are our recommended methods to ensure that water is safe to drink. It is also wise to strain your water before boiling – using a coffee strainer or straining through pairs of tights or stockings will remove most particulate. Allow the water to sit so that small pieces of sediment settle on the bottom.

The Ministry continues to keep the provision of clean drinking water for citizens as its top priority at this time, but until this work is completed, these precautions will keep you safe. If you are in one of the areas which has had clean drinking water supplies restored, you will already know how lucky you are and how we have all learned once more to appreciate as a luxury what once seemed ordinary.

PRIORITIZING FOODSTUFFS

If you're lucky, you may find yourself in a situation where you are able to choose between different foods to scavenge. Of course, you may not be so lucky! If you only have pretzels and canned clams available, that's what you'll be eating until you manage to find other food. (Many a survivor has a tale of an unlikely food combination that kept them going . . . or will never be able to stomach a pretzel or canned clam again in their lives.)

However, you might discover a supermarket with working refrigeration or a well-stocked home or farm which has only recently been abandoned. If you are under heavy attack and have to be on the move shortly, pick the foods which have the lowest weight-to-caloric-value ratio; these will be mostly dried foods and high-fat foods: nuts, seeds and jerky are always good options.

If you don't have to be on the run immediately, however, and can take time choosing between the foods on offer, always use available food resources in the order on page 166.

A NOTE ON JUNK FOOD

Think of your favourite snack food.
Write its name here:

In all probability, over the next ten years you will encounter fewer than 500 pieces of this food. Even when the Ministry's farms begin producing manufactured foods again, crisps, chocolate, biscuits and the like will be low on our priority list for decades to come. Highly processed foods may not be produced again in your lifetime.

You should think about how best to manage this. Consider your favourite junk food. How will you savour it? Which special days will you decide can be marked by eating the kind of sweet foods you love? Will you host a get-together with friends where you can all share your favourite treat? Or will you keep it for a private celebration, closing your eyes as you enjoy the flavour?

We suggest you make a small calendar for yourself on the page opposite, planning your enjoyment of this treat over the next year. It is important, even during dark times such as these, to have something to look forward to. Remember that our ancestors ate sweet foods such as cakes only on high days and holy days. This much can be said for the zombie apocalypse: few of us will take luxuries for granted ever again.

TREAT TIME!

Date	Reason for celebrating	Planned treat

PRIORITY ORDER FOR USING FOOD

FRESH FOODS

These are always top of the list. Fresh foods, whether that is meat, fish, vegetables, fruit or dairy produce, have the highest nutritional content and are also going to go off rapidly! If they are still fresh and haven't spoiled, use them immediately. Don't leave them to rot while you cook pasta. If you have a supply of fresh food (or frozen food) available, always eat it in preference to anything else.

TINNED AND BOTTLED FOODS

Food in tins or glass jars is often of very high nutritional quality but it is heavy to carry. You don't know when you might have to move on. If you have a selection of canned vegetables, beans, pulses, fish or other protein, eat those once the fresh food is gone.

DRIED FOOD

Dried foods are often light enough to carry but they can also take considerable energy to make edible by cooking. (Having said this, in a life-or-death situation it is often possible to rehydrate dried food such as pasta using cold water; experiment with care and never eat dried pulses and beans without boiling them.) If you are in a secure encampment, you may be able to make a fire and cook, but you may also draw zombies to you. Use the smallest flame possible to cook your dried foods, if necessary.

JUNK FOOD

Only eat these foods as a last resort. Not only are biscuits, crisps, chocolate and so on extremely nutrient-poor, and likely to hamper your survival efforts for this reason, they will also be extraordinarily rare for the remainder of your lifetime.

FORAGING

As for our early ancestors, a key way for us to find food today is to forage for it. We forage in supermarkets and in other people's kitchens. But we also forage in the natural world, which is encroaching more and more every day.

We would encourage our readers to attempt to find a copy of the naturalist Richard Mabey's book *Food For Free*, which is a full guide to safely identifying edible species with suggestions for how to cook them. On no account should you attempt to gather wild mushrooms for food without having a knowledgeable fungus expert in your party – many poisonous species look very similar to edible species. Some species, such as the puffball mushroom, are fairly easy to identify after educating yourself, but in general, if you gather mushrooms, it should be purely as a matter of scientific curiosity, to attempt to identify them using a gazetteer and then dispose of them safely. It would take many years of study to be able to accurately identify every species you may come across.

However, some edible plant species that you can feel confident in picking and eating and which grow plentifully in the UK are:

Nettles. Pick them wearing gloves, wash them carefully and pour boiling water over them to remove much of the sting. They can be turned into a delicious soup with the addition of some onions, leeks or garlic, and cook much like spinach with a dash of cream or a splash of oil.

Blackberries. They grow wild on bushes from late summer – start to look for them in July. Wild blackberries can be turned into jam and potted to provide a source of vitamins and minerals through the winter.

Elderflower. Both blossoms and berries can be eaten – the blossoms are delicious coated in batter and fried, and the elderberries can also be turned into wine, if you have enough brewing know-how! Be cautious, however; unripe berries and all green parts of the plant are poisonous.

Nasturtium. A common garden flower. Both the leaves and the petals can be eaten and make a welcome addition to a salad, with a light peppery flavour.

There are many hundreds more edible species growing plentifully in the UK. You would be well advised to allot at least one member of your party to studying the possible sources of wild food near you, to begin to expand your food supplies. And of course remember that every foraging party must leave one person on alert to watch for zombie attack!

FORAGING IN OTHER PEOPLE'S KITCHENS

The Ministry estimates that the food stored in the empty kitchens of the dead would be enough, by itself, to feed the living in the UK for 13 years. The houses of the dead, if they are safe, are a bountiful source of food that should be used.

Firstly, pick your house with care. Suburban and country houses are likely to yield more bountiful larders than small urban apartments, where the residents probably ate meals out in restaurants more often than cooking at home. We estimate that a small party of four or five could tackle one side of a suburban street's kitchens in a day and harvest enough food to feed a small settlement for four weeks.

The second rule of foraging in abandoned houses is to ensure that they are in fact abandoned. Look and listen for signs of other humans and for zombies. Check to see if windows and doors are locked. Kitchens usually face the back of the house and are almost always on the ground floor.

Identify the kitchen. Make a little noise – throw stones against the windows – and see if you attract any humans or undead. Typically, an undead family can be dealt with swiftly and effectively by a party of survivors without much risk of injury.

Your fastest runner should break open the door with a crowbar and then immediately run away from the house to a designated 'trap site' where the shambling dead can be dispatched with axes and – if there is time – laid to rest in their own garden.

Station one member of your party at the kitchen door to keep watch while the others gather food from the kitchen as swiftly as possible. Do not become so distracted that you fail to notice a zombified children's birthday party approaching from the lounge, or a zombie business meeting descending from the upstairs home office.

Do not attempt to open the refrigerator. Contaminants from rotted food are unpleasant and there's some chance that some airborne mould might make one of your party ill.

Strip the kitchen, using the priority list of foods on page 166. Look out for canned goods, dried foods, pulses, pasta, oils, wine, bottled foods, herbs and spices. When you have stripped the kitchen, spray the symbol of a circle bisected by a diagonal line (it should look like a 'zero') to indicate to other survivors that there is no more food here.

Ensure that you bring with you some means of transporting the food that you gather back to your settlement. Supermarket shopping trolleys or wheeled suitcases are ideal for this purpose. If you come under zombie attack on your return journey, do not hesitate to abandon the trolley or case; you can always return later to retrieve it.

FORAGING IN SUPERMARKETS

For some time to come, supermarkets will be an excellent scavenging site for apocalypse survivors. Some – those linked up to solar and wind generators – still have power and may contain edible fresh and frozen foods. Most will still have stocks of canned and dried foods.

However, as many of us have now discovered to our cost, supermarkets can be extremely attractive to zombies. The reasons for this are still unclear – we suspect that zombies are able to perform some actions which they were used to doing very regularly in life. Our current hypothesis is that the idea of 'supermarket' is associated in what remains of the mind of urban zombies with 'food' and that therefore they tend to shamble towards grocery shops in the absence of other stimuli.

This means that any raid on a supermarket must be conducted with extreme vigilance and care. There may be zombies anywhere. They may be in the freezers, or in a storeroom. They may be hiding beneath an upturned shelving unit or behind a display of cereal boxes. Any time you go inside a supermarket, you must have a plan, you must prioritize your supply needs and you must be ready to run at a moment's notice.

We suggest that you follow this procedure every time you go into a supermarket – even one which you know to be safe. There is no time for you to become distracted by bright displays or to reminisce about the days when a 'special offer' meant something.

When you enter the supermarket, set a stopwatch, if you have one. Aim to spend no more than ten minutes grabbing what you need.

Work by priority ordering. First, take any still edible fresh or frozen produce: vegetables, fruits, meat, fish, eggs, dairy. Then, take canned, bottled and dried nutrient-rich foods: pulses, beans, canned fish, canned fruits and vegetables; then oils, herbs and spices, and durable staples: good-quality pasta, rice and flour.

When the timer goes off, you must stop selecting produce immediately. You must accustom yourself to being willing to leave while there are still things you want. This habit may save your life someday.

Do not run. Walk briskly. You cannot afford to fall over in a supermarket – you do not know where a crawler may be lurking.

Many of us wish that we could go back to the time before now and accustom ourselves to behaving in a very different way in supermarkets and around groceries than we did before. Not only would it have improved our health, but by reducing our attachment to shopping as a leisure activity we would have found it easier to adapt to our current circumstances.

HOW TO USE CANNED FOODS

If you have a fire and a variety of canned foods, your options for cooking in an early apocalypse situation are almost limitless. Try these quick, easy and nutritious recipes to improve your canned-food cooking repertoire:

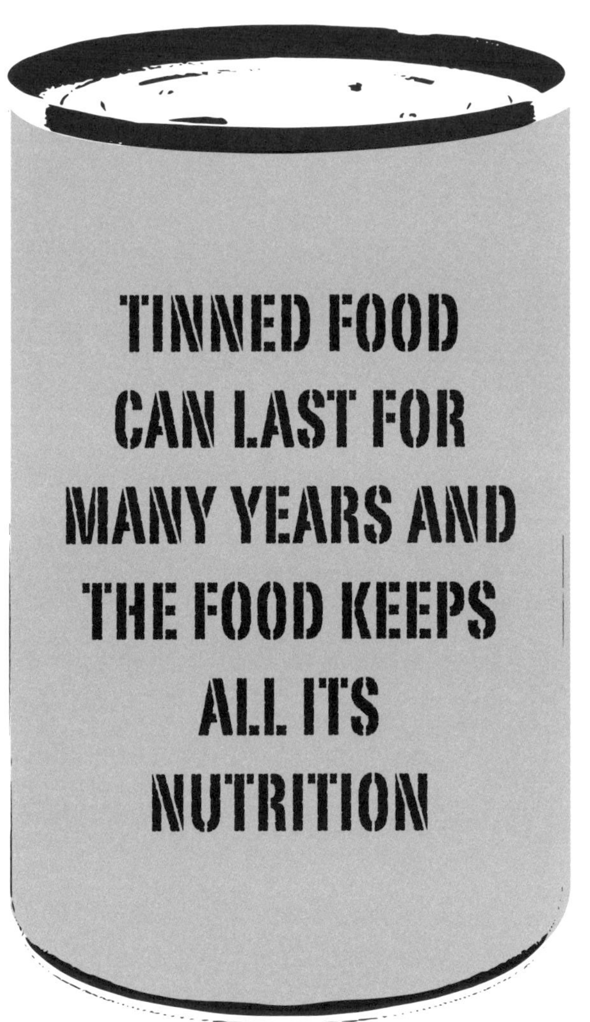

TINNED FOOD
CAN LAST FOR
MANY YEARS AND
THE FOOD KEEPS
ALL ITS
NUTRITION

SPICY CHICKPEAS

Into a pan, empty two cans of chickpeas, one can of fried onions and one can of chopped tomatoes; add a good slug of olive or other cooking oil and a spoonful of harissa (if you can find a jar of this North African spice paste). Add a cup of red wine if you have one. Simmer slowly for half an hour or so, until the liquid has reduced into a thick, glossy sauce. Serve with grated cheese, if you have it. This recipe can be made with any canned beans or pulses.

QUICK AND EASY CHILLI

Into a pan, empty two cans of kidney beans, one can of fried onions, one can of ratatouille if you can find it, or a can of chopped tomatoes, one can of chopped carrots, one can of mushrooms and one can of sweetcorn. Add a good slug of cooking oil, and any form of chilli you can find: if you have a jar of jalapeño peppers, use some of those, but chilli paste, chilli oil, cayenne pepper or chilli flakes will do equally well to add some heat to the dish. Add them gradually so that you can assess how hot they are! Simmer for around an hour to allow the flavours to mingle. This can be served with grated cheese, avocado slices, sour cream and bread, if you are lucky enough to have any of those.

LANCASHIRE HOTPOT

Into a pan, empty two or three cans of boiled potatoes, one can of fried onions and one can of chopped carrots; add a good dash of Worcestershire sauce, if you can find it. Add a good slug of cooking oil and any canned meat you can find, cut into pieces if necessary – you may find the traditional British Spam, which has sustained generations of people in the UK through times of war! This canned meat product can be cut into pieces and added to the stew. If you can't find any canned meat, alternatives include any canned soup that contains meat, or canned German sausages. Add herbs if you can find them: a bay leaf, thyme, garlic or just a dash of mixed herbs. Cook slowly for an hour or so until the flavours have mingled and the juices have formed a rich gravy.

HUNTING AND TRAPPING

Human beings have hunted and trapped animals for food for millennia, and the hunting and trapping methods are far beyond the scope of this book. We advise t. any of these books while scavenging in a library or bookshop you should pick them be worth more to you in the long term than another few tins of food.

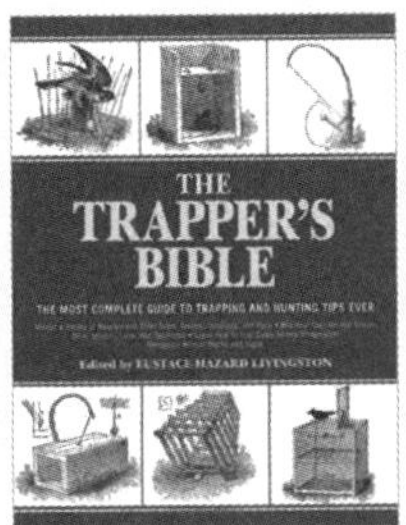

THE TRAPPER'S BIBLE: THE MOST COMPLETE GUIDE TO TRAPPING AND HUNTING TIPS EVER
JAY MCCULLOUGH

THE COMPLETE GUIDE TO HUNTING, BUTCHERING AND COOKING WILD GAME
STEVEN RINELLA

AIR RIFLE HUNTING THROUGH THE SEASONS: A GUIDE TO FIELDCRAFT
MATHEW MANNING

MY LIFE WITH THE ESKIMO
VILHJALMUR STEFANSSON

We also recommend *H is for Hawk* by Helen Macdonald, which will introduce you to some of the intricacies of hunting with wild birds – this is a skill which has been practised for centuries in Europe and which you could consider as a potential way to supplement your food supply, if you have any affinity with it.

For most people, the most important skill to become familiar with is that of setting a basic snare or trap. The 'deadfall' trap is the most simple – a box or heavy stone is balanced on a stick, which is attached by a cord to a piece of bait, in such a way that when the animal moves the bait the stick shifts and the rock or box falls.

We advise caution in setting traps and snares because of the inevitable danger that a zombie may become caught in your trap. A trapped zombie, moaning loudly, may attract a large horde of other zombies. A trapped crawler under your box or stone may pose a danger to you. Therefore it is most advisable to set smaller snares, and to set them at some distance from your dwelling place. Visit your traps regularly – at least once a day – and be prepared to dispatch any zombies there quickly, to avoid attracting a horde.

COOKING SQUIRREL

Wild squirrels are plentiful and an excellent source of protein. Add to this the fact that the grey squirrel is an invasive species in the UK and it is obvious that we should have been hunting, trapping and eating grey squirrel for decades in this country.

A simple baited trap will suffice to catch an ordinary grey squirrel – the animals are very curious and often unafraid of humans. Ministry Briefing no. 87: Squirrel Nutkin: A Useful Food Source contains details of how to construct several useful traps, or the food-related books in the list on page 173 will give some advice.

Wild squirrels should be killed by cranial dispatch. Bullets cannot be wasted on this purpose. Place a sack at the entrance to the trap, baited with food to encourage the animal to move into the sack. Close the sack securely and tip the squirrel into one corner. Put your foot – wear boots – over the squirrel, and deliver a single hard blow to the head with a solid object such as a cosh or large stone. Fortunately, most of us are used to dispatching far more distressing quarry cranially in these difficult times.

Squirrel must be skinned and its organs must be removed before cooking. It can be treated like rabbit for cooking purposes, but remember that the bones are very small – eat with care and use your fingers; they are better than any other implement for finding bones before you choke on them.

A SIMPLE SQUIRREL RECIPE

Allow one squirrel per person.

In a cooking pot, fry some onions, garlic, leeks or spring onions in oil or butter. Add the squirrels and brown thoroughly – you may like to joint them into forequarters and hindquarters so they fit more easily into your pot. Add some fresh or canned vegetables – we recommend canned or dried mushrooms as a particularly delicious addition. Pour over half a glass of white wine or cider per squirrel and simmer gently. The squirrel will be cooked through in around 45 minutes, although you should keep checking it: if your cooking fire is very hot, the liquid may boil away and need to be replenished.

MY RECIPES

Ingredients:

Method:

Notes:

Ingredients:

Method:

Notes:

MY RECIPES

Ingredients:

Method:

Notes:

Ingredients:

Method:

Notes:

MY RECIPES

Ingredients:

Method:

Notes:

Ingredients:

Method:

Notes:

GROWING FOOD

Throughout history, seeds have been the symbol of hope and new beginnings. If you have stood in a walled garden, knowing that you are safe from zombie incursion, holding packets of these tiny flecks that will grow into year-round sustenance, you will know why the seed has this imaginative power. Seeds of edible plants are among our most cherished resources: when the canned and dried food is gone, it is the product of seeds that will sustain us through the decades ahead.

Seeds are light and easy to carry: if you ever come across packets of seeds while scavenging, do not hesitate. Put them in your pack at once. Even if they are seeds for ornamental plants, you may find that they have some food value: roses, violets, nasturtiums, sunflowers, lavender and many other decorative plants have edible portions and will add zest to your diet. Even if you can't eat them, ornamental plants will encourage bees and other helpful insects to come to your garden, or may attract birds or squirrels that you can trap and eat. In addition, there have been unconfirmed reports that some plant species may deter zombies, or alter their behaviour – although it would be unwise to rely on this as part of a home-defence strategy.

Never throw away the seeds from any edible plant you eat – try to plant them out, even if the species is not native to your region and is unlikely to grow to full size. Even if you can't grow an orange tree, you may be able to use some leaves from a small plant for teas, for example. Every extra element of variety in your diet is worthwhile.

In the time before, a gardener might have been able to secure optimum growing conditions, with various composts for different purposes, polytunnels and watering systems. If you have any such equipment available, do not hesitate to use it! Give your plants their best chance to grow. However, if you are stuck in sub-optimal conditions – perhaps with only a balcony or window box during a siege, or a small walled garden, with seeds that have long passed their recommended use-by date, or seeds that may have been taken from genetically engineered sterile plants – what is your best strategy?

If you suspect you will be moving on soon, and that no other humans will be coming this way again, do not plant your seeds, even if they are already out of date. We suggest that if you know you will be settled for a period of time, you should plant out a small number of seeds in whatever way is likely to give them their best chance at survival – keep as close to the packet's instructions as possible, if you have them.

Keep a meticulous garden book. Draw detailed maps of your garden, even if it is only a few saucepans filled with soil. Record what you planted, on what day and at what depth; record whether the seeds were within their use-by date or not. If you collect seeds in subsequent years, or use more seeds from the same packet, this information about which experiments succeeded or failed will be invaluable. In addition, reviewing and updating these records will provide a useful activity to keep you occupied during the long evenings – some garden books are works of artistic excellence. And should you succumb to the zombie plague yourself, another survivor may find your records and be able to use them to continue your work in securing humanity's long-term future.

You may like to colour this image to help with mindfulness in this difficult time.

MY GARDEN MAP

THE ZOMBIE APOCALYPSE GARDENERS' QUESTION TIME

Q: Can you compost zombie flesh?

Ms EQ of Ealing

A: We understand why this is tempting, Ms EQ! Zombie flesh is freely available, and it seems wasteful simply to burn these bodies in times of want. But unfortunately, burning the bodies really is the best strategy. There's little evidence that the zombie virus survives the final 'death' of the zombie body by much – most entirely 'dead' zombie bodies are no longer infectious within a week of death. But we haven't been able to carry out comprehensive research, and there have been some reports that zombie flesh in a well, for example, is capable of infecting people who drink the water. It's simply too risky to willingly introduce zombie flesh into the food chain. It is best to burn the bodies if at all possible. However, when burned and reduced to ash, there is no need to separate zombie flesh from other wood ash that you might use for compost. So the ash can be used!

Q: Is it safe to eat food grown on land where zombies have previously wandered and/or died?

Mr DD of Caithness

A: We advise sensible precautions in this case, Mr DD. The zombie virus has not been fully studied, but it is extremely unlikely that a zombie simply wandering over your field – or even being decapitated there and spreading some flecks of flesh and blood on to your land – would render it dangerous. If possible, dig out the area where the zombie died and include this earth in the cremation pyre, but don't worry unduly. There are thus far no recorded cases of the zombie virus being transmitted via home-grown food, so the chances of it happening are very small; our advice regarding compost is simply a precaution. However, if your land was heavily infested with buried zombies or crawlers, or if you suspect that some zombies have rotted into your garden or field, it would be wise to mark out that land and allow it to lie fallow for several years before replanting, as grazing pasture or as an orchard, rather than using it for root vegetables, to which some flecks of soil may inevitably adhere!

Q: What is the best way to protect my kitchen garden from zombies? I'm particularly concerned about crawlers – maybe just composed of an arm and a head – which have sometimes burrowed in!

Mrs NP of Bath

A: We quite understand the problem, Mrs NP! Ministry gardeners have often come out in the morning to find that their lettuce is overrun with unpleasant crawlers – they pose comparatively little danger in themselves, but they can do a lot of damage to young plants! Anti-fox and anti-squirrel precautions will serve you very well against crawlers. Cover raised beds with chicken wire. If possible, dig your fences further down into the soil – as much as two or three feet extra below the ground can be necessary, we're afraid. If there are no young children nearby likely to injure themselves, try running nails through some wooden battens and placing them at the edges of the beds – the crawlers are likely to become caught on the nails and can be easily disposed of in the morning. And, of course, make sure you wash your food very thoroughly if you suspect any crawlers have been near it!

PACKED LUNCHES

When you travel, it is as well to bring your own supplies of food. You do not know what dangers you may encounter or how long it might be until you next reach a human settlement.

If you have the means to bake bread, the simple sandwich is, of course, a classic for a reason. Otherwise, equip yourself with a simple container and fill it with leftovers: yesterday's stew or casserole, slices of cheese and pickled cucumbers, a salad of tuna with nasturtium leaves. All that's needed to pack an interesting and varied lunch for yourself is a little imagination.

Our advice above all is to get into the habit of always taking enough food with you so that you won't be hungry while you're out performing your day's tasks. It's easy to lapse into thinking in the ways of the time before – particularly if your foraging was successful the previous day – and imagining that you'll 'just find something'. This is the way to end up miles from home, hungry and tired, with your decision-making and reasoning powers low, deciding that you're going to break into a house that is clearly marked as 'dangerous'. You might be surprised how many zombie fatalities can be chalked up to low blood sugar!

Taking care of yourself means more than learning how to run and hide from zombies, and how to fight them – it also means anticipating that you will need food today, and making sensible choices about what you're going to eat later before you leave home.

PLANNING MEALS

Another useful habit is to regularly – perhaps once a week – take stock of the food available to you and plan what to make out of it.

If a band of hunters come home with a whole deer, or if you happen upon a rapidly defrosting but still-fresh cache of fish, you should of course cook and eat them as quickly as possible, even if this means that there's little variety in your diet for a few days! But outside this kind of situation, a plan will help you to make best use of your available food resources.

Write down all the foods you have that are likely to spoil within the next few days if not consumed, in the order they should be eaten. List the number of meals you are planning for, and the number of people likely to be eating each meal.

Plan a nutritious meal using up your leftovers in the order they'll spoil. This might include turning leftover meat into pies, soups or stews. Leftover vegetables can be cooked in a frittata, in croquettes or added to a thick and hearty soup.

Leftover pasta can be added to a soup or made into a pasta bake, while leftover rice should be used within 24 hours but can be turned into a rice bake, arancini or – again! – added to a soup. These are only a few suggestions: the possibilities are endless.

List ideal supplementary ingredients for each of these meals, in order of priority, and give them to every runner going out from your community.

It is vital that we don't waste food. Bones and vegetable peelings can be turned into stock – and the leftover vegetables from those stocks can then be composted! Animals should be eaten nose-to-tail; the dried ends of cheese and bread can be turned into croutons or bases for pies; even the cooking water from pasta contains some nutrition and should be included in soups! But we at the Ministry know that we hardly need to mention this – anyone who's experienced a prolonged siege will never waste a scrap of food again.

FOOD THAT NEEDS EATING

Food	Eat by:

WEEKLY MEAL PLAN

Monday	
Tuesday	
Wednesday	
Thursday	
Friday	
Saturday	
Sunday	

FOOD PRESERVATION

We can no longer rely on refrigeration. If you have a solar-, wind- or generator-powered refrigerating unit, you are exceptionally fortunate.

Therefore it is important to become familiar with various methods of preserving foods. Again, this book will hardly suffice to cover the many ways to preserve food that humanity has developed over the centuries. There are many competent articles on the subject on ROFFLENET, and many books to consult.

We suggest that a good place to begin would be to learn the arts of smoking and drying meat and fish and fruits, and learning to make preserves from gluts of fruits and vegetables. Many of us would agree that these foods can be even tastier than the fresh varieties, and if you have a fire in your hearth – as most of us do these days – you are already producing 'waste energy' that could be put to good use smoking your food.

One important consideration is that zombies are attracted by the scent of raw meat. In general, zombies prefer to 'eat' the flesh of living humans – of course their digestive systems no longer work, so they're not really eating the flesh; they're attracted to humans in order to bite and infect us with their pathogen. But we suspect that the smell of other mammal flesh in particular is similar enough to human flesh to confuse them. Zombies don't chase other living animals, but they've sometimes been observed feasting on the carcass of a dead horse or dog.

The Ministry has never received any report of zombies being attracted to the scent of fish. Therefore, drying and smoking salmon or trout is likely to pose no risk, even if the scent carries for a long distance. You should take great precautions, however, when smoking animal meat – do not attempt it on an open fire, or in an unprotected spot. Do not leave meat out overnight. Do not leave its blood or viscera near your home – aim to eat absolutely every edible part of the animal, and if some has to be discarded, leave it far away from your dwelling place.

MINISTRY FARMS

If you're without a community, or if you simply want to become involved in rebuilding our country in a tangible way, why not come to live and work at a Ministry of Recovery farm?

We are working together to secure a safe water supply for our people and to create new sustainable farming methods for the new era. Our projects include:

- Recovering polytunnel technology to grow a variety of tropical fruits in the UK – there is every chance that many of us will taste a banana again in our lifetimes!
- Growing and hybridizing new hardy strains of crops; we are particularly in need of agricultural specialists, but all hands are welcome.
- Rescuing and rehousing farm animals which may have been left to run wild since the apocalypse; many food-animal populations experienced significant suffering after the sudden death of those people who were farming them. We are working to create re-wilded UK populations of boar, goat, sheep, deer and bison, and smaller populations of domesticated pigs, sheep, cows and poultry.
- The safe disposal of zombie bodies, and their processing into ash-fertilizer for the soil.
- Many more projects, including those which perhaps you will suggest to us! We're always open to new and innovative ideas, and we want to hear from all our citizens.

COME ALONG TO YOUR NEAREST MINISTRY OF RECOVERY FARM AND, AFTER A SHORT TIME IN QUARANTINE, YOU'LL BE MET WITH OPEN ARMS!

CASE STUDY Sam Yao

I can't tell a lie. Before the apocalypse I was a junk-food addict. There are just so many nummy treats, man. I mean, I can't even ... Do you remember Caramacs? And those little crispy triangle things? Moments? Minutes? Doesn't matter. We all have something we remember and love. And obviously, like a lot of people in Britain, the idea that one day we might run out of Marmite makes me want to curl up into a ball and cry.

But since the apocalypse I've had to branch out into non-junk-food alternatives. I've thought a lot about how there'll come a day when there are just no more Curly Wurlies left. Like, it's OK. I've made my peace with it. But when that day comes, I don't want to be looking back and remembering times that I made myself sick by eating too many. I want to remember the good times. Savouring every bite, making it count. Every time I have a Curly Wurly now, it's an event for me. Sometimes I'll eat it alone, sometimes shared with friends. It makes me feel good to know that I've taken a few minutes to really enjoy it.

Other than that, I think the most important thing is to be able to eat a real variety of foods. For me, that's meant learning to like food I thought I hated. Did you know that if there's a food you hate, you can usually make yourself like it by trying a tiny bite about once every two or three weeks, six or seven times? It actually works! I never thought I liked chicory – bitter nasty flavour – but we grow a lot of it here at Abel so I decided I should try to enjoy it. After giving it a go a few times now, I actually look forward to that bitter flavour! I'm as surprised as you are, man.

And that's the thing: in the zombie apocalypse we've all had to learn to do stuff that we never thought we could. And in the process, we've learned to like stuff that we never thought we would. Maybe it's you, learning that you can actually make a mean zombie-defence shelter out of four camp beds and some elastic ropes. Or maybe you've learned that you can do more physically than you thought: walking, running, throwing, sticking your axe into a zombie's head. Or maybe you've found new skills in, like, listening to people, or making tactical plans, or like me, just talking on the radio.

That's the whole of it, isn't it? Maybe we could always have done more than we thought. But we didn't have to. And now we've had to ... I think we've all learned to respect ourselves more. Look at me. Look at you. The apocalypse was terrible. Is terrible. But what we've learned to do: that's been amazing.

‘IN THE ZOMBIE APOCALYPSE WE’VE ALL HAD TO LEARN TO DO STUFF THAT WE NEVER THOUGHT WE COULD.’

NOTES

SECTION 07

YOUR MINISTRY AND YOU

KEEPING FIT WHILE WORKING FOR THE MINISTRY

You may already have been assigned work by a local representative of the Ministry of Recovery. Perhaps you spend your days much as you did in the time before – sitting behind an office desk, retrieving old files and salvaging information, cataloguing books, reading and studying technical manuals or performing administrative duties. Perhaps you are lucky enough to be employed in a zombie-free fenced-off zone. Maybe you feel that some of our recommendations for health and fitness do not apply to you.

We would encourage you not to think in this way. You never know when you might encounter a zombie, and the zombie-apocalypse-fit routine is one you can incorporate into your day, for life, whatever your circumstances. Pack your lunch as if you were about to venture out into the wilderness and you'll never lose your skills. Use your journey to and from your work to practise your surveillance and to improve your fitness. Take a ten-minute break from your desk to perform some simple callisthenics, such as the exercises on page 20. None of these measures need be time-consuming or heroic; a short routine which you can reliably perform most days is better than a long and time-consuming one that you'll actually get to only once a fortnight! Remember what happened to so many people in those dreadful first days of the apocalypse and set up a plan for yourself which will leave you ready to act in the event of a zombie emergency.

OUR PLAN FOR BRITAIN'S FUTURE

There is no doubt that this disease has been the greatest blow the UK – and the human world – has ever suffered. But it is not the end of us.

We do not intend to go back to the world as it was in the time before. We think this is an opportunity to make a better society for all of us.

As we have tried to communicate through this book, the zombie apocalypse is not like other wars and disasters humanity has faced. The strongest of us are not necessarily those who have survived. The zombie virus does not favour those who isolate themselves, or those who are willing to kill other humans to attain advantage. It favours the skilful, the thoughtful, those who plan strategically and are able to work cooperatively with others.

We think this holds out a great deal of hope for the future of the human race after the last zombie is defeated, the last body is burned and the last groaning moan has faded from memory.

We have the scientific and technical knowledge of the time before to work with; we live on a planet which is already repairing itself from ecological disaster. We believe that, working together in villages and small townships, we can build a better and more sustainable way of life for human beings.

THIS IS NOT THE END OF US

It has seemed to be the end many times. The Black Death seemed to be an end. Bubonic plague seemed to be the end. Many of us thought that environmental disaster would be the end.
But here we are.

In these dark times, it is important to ask ourselves what makes the human race worth fighting for. We cannot tell you what that is for you. We can tell you what it is for us. We have seen individual acts of such heroism and courage that we will never lose faith entirely in humanity. We have saved from destruction works of art of staggering beauty, pieces of music of vitality and brilliance, literature that calls us to purposes higher than ourselves. We are the only species known in the universe to have penetrated the mysteries of DNA, of quantum mechanics, to have sent a living creature from Earth to the moon.

The human race is – we contend – one of the most beautiful things this planet has ever produced. You are part of that. That is why you are worth fighting for.

'EVERY DAY, YOU MAY SEE SOME SMALL IMPROVEMENT. EVERY DAY, YOUR HARD WORK AFFIRMS YOUR COMMITMENT TO YOURSELF, AND TO THE HUMAN RACE. YOU WILL NEVER REACH PERFECTION; THERE IS NO SUCH THING.

WE WILL NOT SEE THE END OF THIS JOURNEY, FOR THERE IS NO END TO THE JOURNEY, ONLY A PATH OF CONTINUAL SMALL CHANGES. THERE WILL ALWAYS BE MORE WE CAN STRIVE FOR. BUT FAR FROM DISHEARTENING US, THIS KNOWLEDGE ONLY ADDS SATISFACTION AND RELISH TO OUR WORK.'

APPENDIX A

RADIO OPERATED FREE FORM LINKLAYER EMERGENCY NETWORKING (ROFFLENET)

BY ALEX MACMILLAN

APPENDIX A

The ROFFLENET is a blueprint for a global network of radio-connected devices capable of replacing the Internet in case of massive infrastructure failure (in particular, the failure of the Internet's core routers and Internet service providers due to widescale power loss or otherwise).

ROFFLENET is an agreed protocol on how geeks with ham radio hardware should coordinate to establish low-data-rate radio networks (lolnets) which can then be interconnected in order to build a global data system. It is assumed that the geeks constructing the ROFFLENET will not be able to move freely, preventing them from meeting one another, or exchanging hardware or software on physical media.

TERMINOLOGY

Cantenna: a jury-rigged antenna, commonly built from a Pringles can, or paper and tin foil. Essential for converting weak omnidirectional antennas (such as those found on cheap WiFi access points) into directional antennas that can be used to establish point-to-point links over longer distances.

DTE (Data Terminal Equipment): a generic term for any device which connects a computer to a data service. Joining ROFFLENET is mostly about building a working DTE and connecting it to a peer.

Ham modem: a ham radio that has been converted to act as a DTE, allowing a computer to send and receive data to and from ROFFLENET. The ham modem doesn't handle digital signals, but it does handle the job of modulating a computer's baseband signal on to an antenna, and demodulating the received signal to a baseband signal that can be decoded by a computer.

ADC (Analogue to Digital Conversion) and DAC (Digital to Analogue Conversion): ADC and DAC convert analogue signals into digital streams of ones and zeros, and vice versa. This is the step that turns a baseband signal into useful data. Packet radios in mobile phones have dedicated, high-quality (but inaccessible) integrated ADCs and DACs. Fortunately, high-quality ADCs and DACs can also be found on virtually every sound card on the planet, and sound cards are very easy to manipulate into encoding and decoding analogue audio signals for and from ham modems using popular programming languages like Python and C.

SDR Software Defined Radio (aka GNU Radio and Universal Radio): the practice of building high-bandwidth DTEs that demodulate radio signals in software instead of using tuned hardware components. SDRs are capable of much higher bandwidth communication than ROFFLENET ham modems, but the required equipment is harder to find, and they are more difficult to build and configure.

APPENDIX A

Cognitive modem (aka bacon modem): an SDR that is operated with a cognitive radio protocol, enabling considerably higher-rate data connections to ROFFLENET. Cognitive radio protocols automatically select frequencies for communication, which provides considerable benefits over fixed-frequency ham modems, including reduced interference, automatic contention reduction and MIMO.

While ham modems are an essential first step for connecting to the ROFFLENET, bacon modems actually form the ROFFLENET backbone, handling major crosscountry and sometimes intercountry data flows. In many cases, geeks only operate ham modems so that they can download the software they need to build and operate superior bacon modems.

Lolnet (Local Only Linklayer Networking): a low-rate packet-data network consisting of two or more devices sharing a single radio channel in order to exchange data.

ROFFLENET (Radio Operated Free Form Linklayer Emergency Networking): a worldwide collection of lolnets interconnected by ad hoc routers, with multiple uplinks to (the remains of) the Internet. By using long-distance ham radio and satellite repeaters, it is possible to join ROFFLENET from anywhere in the world (though access speeds may initially be very, very slow).

GBSD (Global Bootstrap Software Delivery): a global lolnet. Geeks who have the hardware but not the software to build a ham modem can write a simple lolnet decoder by hand in C or Python and then connect to the GBSD in order to download the rest of the software that they need. The GBSD is transmitted on a standard schedule and frequency worldwide, using the simplest possible data encoding, and can even be picked up using a passive 'crystal' radio circuit, as found in many children's science kits.

RRS (ROFFLENET Routing Station): a theoretical hub for ROFFLENET communication, consisting of multiple ham and bacon modems interconnected by a ROFFLENET router (and possibly an Internet uplink). Ideally, RRSs are sited at antenna towers.

ROFFLENET geeks at Emley Moor have already designated the Emley Moor tower as 'Narwhal Station'. It is currently routing and providing an Internet uplink for six test lolnets in the Yorkshire area.

Maintaining an RRS is especially challenging because operating multiple high-power radios usually requires a continuously running generator as a power source.

APPENDIX A

Coding rate: an alphanumeric description of the baseband linklayer protocol that is being used to transmit data bits on a given lolnet frequency. It consists of a code length (in bits), an optional channel count and a symbol rate (in Hz or symbols per second). The coding rate descriptor format is:

X[.C].Y

X is the code length;

C is the optional channel count (most lolnets only use a single channel);

Y is the symbol rate, expressed using engineering notation where the exponent symbol is also the decimal point.

For example:

8.1.2K (or just 8.2K) is an 8-bit, single-channel, 2000-symbols-per-second code – offering a maximum data transfer rate of 16kbps.

20.2.192K is a 20-bit, dual-channel, 192,000-symbols-per-second code offering a maximum throughput of 7.68Mbps, or roughly the maximum throughput achievable on any ham lolnet.

2.K2 is a binary, single-channel, 200-symbols-per-second code offering a meagre 400bps. Because of the incredible variance of radio conditions and quality of equipment, coding rates are often chosen by lolnet operators on a case-by-case basis. While the coding rate of a lolnet can be determined simply by tuning to the lolnet and analysing the lolnet signal, it's more common to use the ham radio in voice mode to ask local lolnet operators what coding rates they're using in person.

APPENDIX A

ANATOMY OF A ROFFLENET NODE

The following is a diagram showing the various hardware and software stacks that may be composed to build a functioning ROFFLENET node.

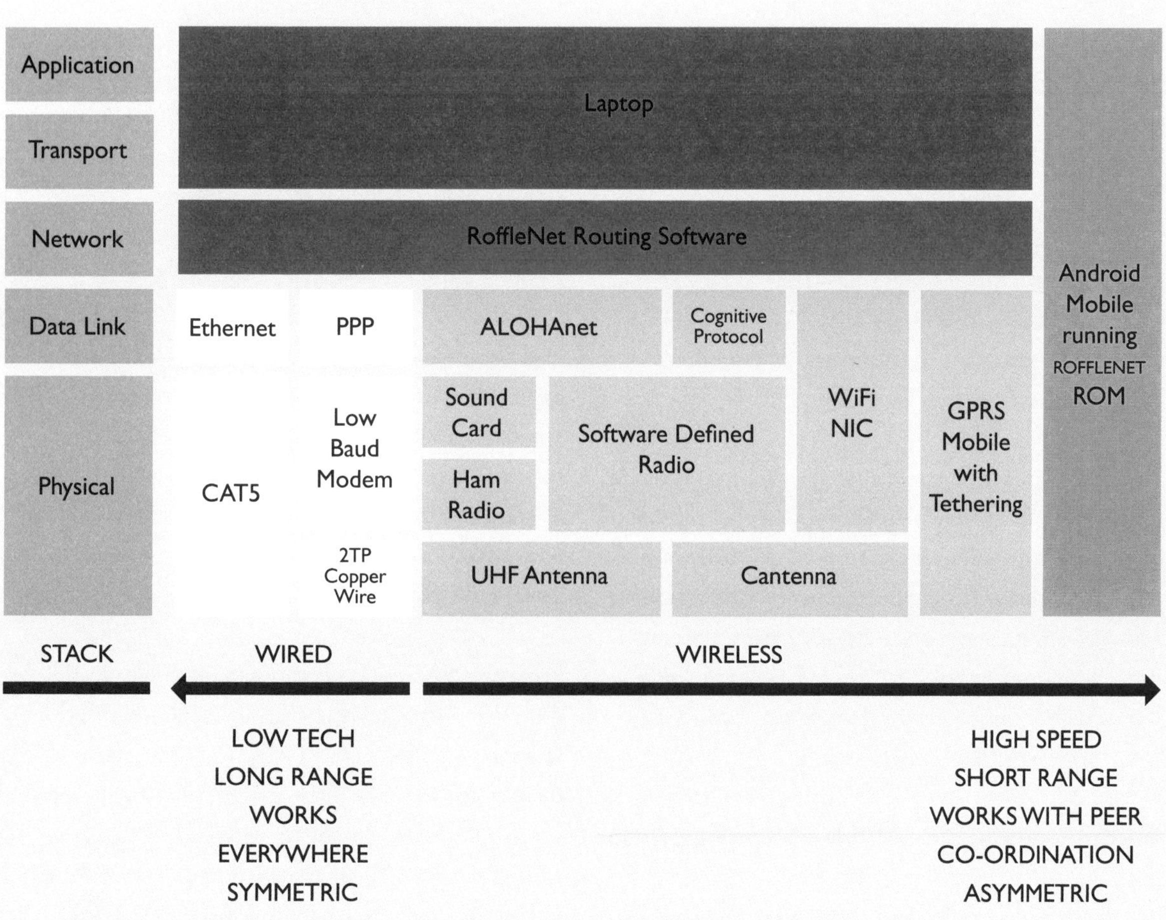

APPENDIX A

YOU WILL NEED:

A two-way radio

You need a radio capable of transmitting and receiving. The quality of your radio will affect the maximum link speed you can attain – broadly speaking, the larger the radio case, the higher the quality of the radio.

Note that standard household radios are very rarely able to transmit, due to their lack of a power amplifier capable of driving the radio antenna.

An antenna

Radios are useless without antennas. Antennas can be made from coat hangers and scrap wire, but the best antennas are carefully designed, built and balanced for the frequency range you intend to transmit and receive at. Read the supporting document 'Antenna Design for Scavengers' for more information. Again, the quality of the antenna will directly impact the maximum link speed you can attain.

A laptop with 'line in' and 'line out' audio sockets

Your laptop sound card acts as the analogue-to-digital and digital-to-analogue converter. Better sound cards will be able to attain higher link speeds.

A typical laptop sound card has a 10-bit resolution with a 44100 Hz baud rate on two channels, giving a theoretical maximum data rate through your ham modem of 0.8Mbps (10.2.44K1); however, this is only ever achievable with top-quality radio hardware and a close to perfect radio link.

Most lolnets are run with a 'safe' QPSK 4-bit symbol code on a single channel and a baud rate of around 4000 symbols per second (4.4K), giving a typical data rate of 16kbps (minus error correction and overhead). This 'safe' data rate makes it easier for new hams to join the lolnet with less than ideal hardware.

In extremely challenging radio environments, lolnets can be operated at just 2-bit resolution (usually BPSK) and symbol rates as low as 200 baud (2.K2). This means just 400bps, which nonetheless is still enough to send and receive email, and to receive close to real time bulletin updates from ROFFLENET news services. The GBSD lolnet is run at 2.K2.

Professional sound recording and playback hardware can offer higher quality ADCs and DACs, which can speed up your access to a ham lolnet (as long as all peers can handle the higher data rate as well). Typical values for professional audio hardware are a 20-bit resolution and 192kHz sample rate on two channels, raising the theoretical limit to 7.6Mbps (20.2.192K). Narwhal Station has successfully operated a point-to-point lolnet with Black Hill Station in Scotland at around 6Mbps using DACs and ADCs from MAudio's professional hardware range.

APPENDIX A

HOW TO...

Contact a ROFFLENET ham operator

You should scan the ham radio frequencies for transmissions from other ham users. If scanning is difficult, tune to the ROFFLENET 'hello' voice frequency and make regular transmissions until another ham replies.

If you don't already have the ROFFLENET software

Build your ham radio receiver

Follow instructions in the ROFFLENET Hardware Guide.

Connect to the GBSD

The GBSD transmits at 800kHz using amplitude modulation (AM) with no sideband. The GBSD transmission begins at 20 minutes past the hour, every hour. Medium wave (MW) signals propagate further after sunset. Due to its simple coding scheme, in audio mode the GBSD is identifiable by its characteristic monotonic buzzing drone.

Download the ROFFLENET software

Your decoder should detect the start of the transmission and then begin outputting the contents of the bootstrap software. Roughly 200 kilobytes of software is included in the bootstrap package, so the GBSD transmission lasts a little under ten minutes.

You should verify that you downloaded the GBSD correctly by calculating the MD5 sum of the received data – the expected MD5 hash is included in the download.

Set up your ROFFLENET ham modem

Follow instructions in the ROFFLENET Hardware Guide.

Join a local UHF lolnet frequency

You can scan for 4.4K lolnets in your area and use the ROFFLENET probe to see if you are able to decode any data, or use the usual ham frequencies to ask ROFFLENET operators in your area what channels are in use.

Ping a peer

Once you've found a lolnet with your ham radio, start the lolnet driver and attempt to ping any IP addresses that the ROFFLENET probe reports in the traffic.

Ping Narwhal Station

If the lolnet is connected to ROFFLENET, you should be able to ping Narwhal Station at its static IP address 70.55.13.1.

Configure DNS

You should use a DNS server on or close to your lolnet, if available. If not, use Narwhal Station's DNS servers at 70.55.13.10 and 70.55.13.11.

CONGRATULATIONS! YOU'RE CONNECTED TO ROFFLENET.

FIXED FREQUENCIES

800 kHz	2.K2 GBSD
5000 kHz	ROFFLENET ham 'hello' voice channel
8000 kHz	Narwhal Station's 2.K2 wide-area general bulletin frequency – you should not transmit on this frequency
8080 kHz	A popular 4.4K lolnet testing frequency – interference and hidden-terminal issues are likely but it's often a useful starting point.

TROUBLESHOOTING

My computer is running Windows

You are basically stuffed. It's virtually impossible to write a GBSD downloader in a stock Windows installation. Your best bet is to get a runner to fetch a USB Linux distribution from a nearby ham.

If you happen to have any development tools installed on your Windows machine, you may still be able to write a GBSD decoder. A compiled Windows binary of the ROFFLENET tools is broadcast on Thursdays at 1835 UTC.

I don't have a ham radio

Being able to transmit is a more or less essential part of participating on ROFFLENET; however, even without a transmitter you may benefit from being able to read traffic on lolnets in your area. You may as well download the GBSD anyway, and use the ROFFLENET probe to look for and capture traffic on local lolnets – you may find you are able to access regular bulletins if a lolnet peer is already requesting them, and you'll be ready to join ROFFLENET for real as soon as you acquire a usable transmitter.

NOTES

NOTES

APPENDIX B

A SPOTTER'S GUIDE TO ZOMS

BY MATT WIETESKA

APPENDIX B

BURIED ZOMS

The least mobile zoms, but that doesn't make them any less dangerous. Most likely to be found in areas which have recently experienced significant landfall or around collapsed buildings. In these areas, ensure that you check your route carefully as you proceed. Remember: being surprised is deadly. Engage buried hostiles by assessing their range of movement from a safe distance, identifying a safe angle of approach, and then terminating them as safely as possible.

CRAWLERS

Many zoms have lost the ability to use their legs, but remain mobile by crawling. They can be easily outrun, but are still dangerous at close quarters, as they are capable of leaping across distances of up to five feet in order to engage.

Best termination practice

Working in a pair
Runner A maintains a safe distance while distracting the zom's attention.

Runner B flanks the zom and engages to terminate from behind, ensuring no contamination reaches Runner A.

When solo
Find an upward slope or staircase to minimize the zom's ability to engage you from a distance.

Entice the zom to leap while avoiding its attack.

As the zom lands, it is vulnerable.

Move in swiftly and strike.

SHAMBLERS

The most common zom. They're capable of moving around normal walking speed, but move with a distinctive 'shambling' gait. Outrunning a lone shambler is well within your capabilities. However, in groups, they can present a significant danger due to their tenacity and ability to swamp a runner with their numbers.

Best termination practice

Working in a pair
Runner A maintains a safe distance while distracting the zom's attention.

Runner B flanks the hostile and engages to terminate from one side, ensuring no contamination reaches Runner A.

When solo

Use an upward slope, as above, to gain a mobility advantage over the zom before terminating opportunistically

OR

Find a bottleneck or choke point, allowing you to dispatch zoms one by one, should their numbers present a problem.

SPRINTERS

Mercifully rare, these zoms are capable of speeds to rival most runners. When encountering a sprinter, escape should be your first priority. Use all techniques at your disposal to gain and maintain a lead on the hostile. In particular, look for upward slopes, uneven ground, or loose stones. While sprinters are capable of matching pace with most runners, they lack intelligence and environmental awareness. Use this to your advantage. If you are unable to escape a sprinter, seek a vantage point from which to engage and terminate. Again, safety should be your priority here, but it is likely that you will need to resort to less favourable methods in order to gain an upper hand.

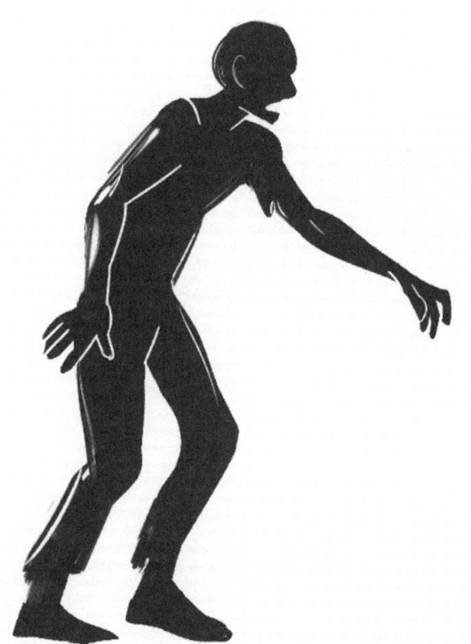

ACKNOWLEDGEMENTS

Zombies, Run! has been a collaborative project since that first day when Naomi Alderman and Adrian Hon came up with the idea together. So, we really have more people to thank than we can fit into a book.

For starters, thanks to the original core ZR team, those who were there at the very start and made that Kickstarter project happen: Estée Chan, Alex Macmillan and Matt Wieteska. Thanks to all the team at Six to Start who've worked on making the game, in the past and the present. Thanks to all our Kickstarter backers, and to our amazing community of players, whose emails and tumblr posts and fanfic inspire us every day. Stay safe out there, all you Runners Five.

Thanks to Kascha Sweeney for the fantastic illustrations, and for her design work on the book.

Thanks to our incredible cast who have brought the ZR characters to life, in particular to Philip Nightingale, Jennifer Tan, Victoria Grove, Sally Orrock, Clare Kissane and Eleanor Rushton.

Thanks to Penguin, to our agent Veronique Baxter, our editor Emily Robertson and our copy-editor Emma Horton. Thanks to Fiona Silk, who devised some of our exercise plans, and to Dr Nicola Walsh, Associate Professor in Musculoskeletal Rehabilitation at the University of the West of England, who was the medical advisor on this book.

Thanks most of all to you, members of the human race who are not yet zombies. Some days will always feel like the actual zombie apocalypse, but we've seen enough in our lives to believe that the human race is still worth fighting for. And that includes each of us.

NOTES

NOTES

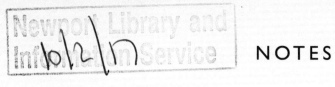